The Pirate Next Door

The Pirate Next Door

*The Untold Story of Eighteenth Century
Pirates' Wives, Families and Communities*

Daphne Palmer Geanacopoulos

CAROLINA ACADEMIC PRESS

Durham, North Carolina

Library of Congress Cataloging-in-Publication Data
Names: Geanacopoulos, Daphne Palmer.
Title: The pirate next door : the untold story of eighteenth century pirates'
  wives, families and communities / Daphne Palmer Geanacopoulos.
Description: Durham, North Carolina : Carolina Academic Press, LLC, 2016. |
  Includes bibliographical references and index.
Identifiers: LCCN 2016036257 | ISBN 9781611638752 (alk. paper)
Subjects: LCSH: Pirates--History--18th century. | Pirates--Social life and
  customs. | Pirates--Social conditions.
Classification: LCC G535 .G42 2016 | DDC 910.4/5--dc23
LC record available at https://lccn.loc.gov/2016036257

CAROLINA ACADEMIC PRESS, LLC
700 Kent Street
Durham, North Carolina 27701
Telephone (919) 489-7486
Fax (919) 493-5668
www.cap-press.com

Printed in the United States of America
2023 Printing

For David, Christina and Danielle

Contents

Author's Note

I would like to thank the following people for their valuable assistance in writing this book: Bethany Bower, Ken Gross, Dennis Todd, Ori Soltes, Colleen Lawrie, Chuck O'Connor, Betsy Griffith Daniel, my uncle, Vernon Valentine Palmer, the late Kenneth J. Kinkor and Betsy Sigman. Sarah Hodge from the New York Public Library, Bert Lippincott, III from the Newport Historical Society, Millie McGinnes from the Block Island Town Clerk's office, Wallace Joiner from the Frist Center for the Visual Arts, Paul Johnson at the Image Library of the National Archives in London, Barry Clifford with the Whydah Pirate Museum, and the staffs at the Rhode Island Historical Society, Massachusetts Archives, and the Manuscripts and Maps Divisions of the Library of Congress were extremely cordial and helpful. A special thank you to my publisher Keith Sipe, Linda Lacy, and his wonderful staff at Carolina Academic Press who made this book possible. Finally, I could not have done without the love and good cheer of my family—my daughters Danielle and Christina, and especially my husband, David.

I would like to add that in the sections where I have quoted from a primary source, I have left the spelling and grammar in its original form to give the reader the full effect of the language of the period.

The Pirate Next Door

Introduction

They have many names—pirates, freebooters, brethren of the coast, members of the company, buccaneers. Throughout the late seventeenth and early eighteenth centuries, thousands of pirates stalked the seas, attacking merchant vessels trading in the West Indies, West Africa, and North America. This period of violence and thievery has been well documented and immortalized as the "Golden Age of Piracy," and even though it has been more than three hundred years since pirates walked the docks of Atlantic seaports, cleaned their vessels in hidden island alcoves, and hoisted their dreaded black flags, these men continue to capture our imagination. Books, novels, plays and movies keep the pirate mythology alive and well in popular culture. But these mediums often present at best a one-dimensional picture, and at worst, a completely inaccurate one of the lives and loves of history's most notorious scoundrels. Whether they are portrayed as romantic outlaws who defied the conventions of their society, or as anti-social villains, the common assumption about pirates is that they were radically individualistic and scornful of the common ties that bind society together. Young, unmarried, unemployed deep-water sailors from the lowest rungs of society, poor and uneducated, pirates were portrayed as social isolates with no connection to society beyond the confines of their ships. In the words of the French historian Hubert Deschamps pirates were:

> ... a unique race, born of the sea and of a brutal dream, a free people, detached from other human societies and from the future, without children and without old people, without homes and without cemeteries, without hope but not without audacity, a people for whom atrocity was a career choice and death a certitude of the day after tomorrow.[1]

3

Though there certainly is some truth in this characterization, it is a gross over-generalization. There are troves of evidence proving that a not insignificant number of these men were married, had strong family ties and connections to a community on land, were educated (at least to some extent) and came from families who enjoyed some degree of status in their respective societies.

It is widely believed that men who turned pirate did so because they were hardened criminals hell-bent on gaining riches. In most cases, this is simply not true. It was often economic and cultural factors that influenced a man's decision to turn pirate.

One major factor was the British trade restrictions in the Navigations Acts. These laws squeezed the economic health out of the colonies. The British crown had an empire to run, and they taxed the colonies both to help them run it and to enrich the mother country. The crown applied mercantilist doctrine to colonial trade by imposing the Navigation Acts of 1660 and 1673. These and several others placed restrictions on what the colonies could manufacture, whose ships they could use and with whom they could do business. They required that all imported goods go by way of England, which added enormously to the cost of transport and depressed the market for North American goods abroad. This caused great tension between Great Britain and the North American colonists, so in 1678 the crown sent an emissary named Edward Randolph to monitor and enforce the trade policies in the colonies. Unsurprisingly, he was not highly regarded by the colonists, who deeply resented the British taxation on them.

The Navigation Acts made it nearly impossible for the merchants to conform to the rules established by the crown and still survive economically so many took matters into their own hands and began smuggling their goods to Europe. To facilitate their illegal activity, they built wharves and warehouses and commissioned the construction of boats to sail to faraway ports. The stronger enforcement of the navigation laws and the resulting trade imbalance meant that there was much less revenue flowing into the colonial economy which created a shortage in the currency of the time—gold and silver coins called *specie.* The combination of ailing economies in the colonies and angry colonists made the climate ripe for a solution that would protect everyone's self-interest. That solution was piracy.

Pirates contributed to the emerging economies of North America by bringing in much-needed gold and silver coins stolen from captured ships called prizes. The silver coins were Spanish dollars called "pieces of eight" that could be cut in up to eight pieces to give change. From distant places they also brought food and luxury items that the colonists were eager to purchase. Because the pirates had little overhead, they were able to sell their goods cheaply to the merchants, and purchase goods from them as well, turning a nice profit in this little micro-economy.[2] Pirates brought money into the communities and employed local mariners, shipbuilders, craftsmen, and suppliers. As an essential part of the economy, pirates were needed and appreciated so the stigma they have now did not really exist then. They were considered heroes. Piracy was a solution to the problem created by the British authorities and for men desperate for work and on the fence about whether to turn pirate, this lackadaisical attitude towards piracy was enough to convince many.

There was another reason men turned to piracy, however. Often, after long periods of warfare ended, naval forces were downsized, leaving many privateers and seamen out of work. This happened following the signing of the Treaty of Utrecht in 1713, which put an end to the thirteen-year War of Spanish Succession in which England, France, and Spain fought over who had the right to succeed Charles II as King of Spain. In England alone, an estimated 40,000 privateers and seamen walked the streets of seaside towns looking for jobs.[3] A privateer and his crew had a privately owned and armed vessel and were contracted by a European government during wartime to capture and seize enemy shipping. The usual terms for a privateer captain and his crew was "no purchase, no pay," which meant that if they did not bring back plunder and prizes, they did not get paid. Privateers provided an important function during wartime, functioning as an auxiliary to the navy.

Pirates, on the other hand, were not legally sanctioned to plunder and seize merchant ships. Each pirate ship operated as an independent entity and the captain and the crew shared all the booty.

Pirates were not loyal to a particular country and they indiscriminately attacked ships of all nations. Privateering was considered legal, while piracy was considered a crime. Though the differences between a privateer and a pirate may seem clear, in practice, it was a complicated system fraught with abuse. In the late seventeenth and eighteenth-century maritime world, a privateer occupied a dubious legal status, being considered no more than a licensed pirate. All too often, however, it was an easy jump from grey area to pirate when unhappy privateer crews argued over the terms in the commission. Many started out as legitimate citizens and ended up as pirates. Privateers and pirates had blurred identities as legitimate and illegitimate businessmen and these men were often welcome (or at least tolerated) members of the community.

Some unemployed privateers and sailors joined the crew of merchant and naval vessels but these captains were often brutally cruel men who wielded violent and arbitrary authority over their crews. Flogging with a cat-o'-nine-tails, sometimes six or seven hundred lashes, and keel-hauling (pulling seamen underneath the ship from one side to the other, often resulting in their early death) were common practices. Conditions onboard the ships were less than tolerable with poor rations and diseases such as scurvy, dysentery and syphilis. And all this usually came with very low pay. Turning pirate was not only a way to escape the harsh conditions, but also to get revenge against those brutal ship captains who had made their lives so miserable.[4] When pirates attacked merchant ships, they took charge of the captain's future. If a captain had been cruel to his crew, he was punished in a way that befitted his crimes.

Piracy was often a direct rebellion against the life the men once knew. "Going on the account" was a term used by pirates that meant that payment was a share of the plunder rather than monthly wages. This was a somewhat risky but often lucrative way for a mariner or a landsmen to make a fortune, or at least support themselves and their families if they had them. In 1709, forty-eight pirate wives and relations of "Pirates and Buccaneers of Madagascar and elsewhere in the East and West Indies" signed a petition asking Queen Anne of England to spare their husbands' lives from the gallows and to allow them to keep their husband's stolen loot.[5]

One may think this petition absurd—a community of wives asking the Queen to pardon their sea-roving, thieving husbands and brothers and allow them to keep their stolen goods—but this plea highlights important sociological and economic considerations not otherwise associated with pirates. These women were committed not only to their husbands but also to the financial security of their families and the loot was family income. What is abundantly clear is that for some men, piracy was a last ditch effort to provide for their families when other legitimate means of employment were limited or nonexistent. The petition also gives lie to the myth that pirates were social isolates who had no human relations beyond those they formed aboard ship. Some pirates, in fact, were just ordinary men with wives and families who chose to engage in a risky and dangerous business that pitted them against the authorities.

Who were these men who turned pirate? They were Europeans—especially English—Native Americans, free Blacks and runaway slaves. On board their ships they spoke many languages and came from many cultures and the pirates did not discriminate because of race, religion or nationality. Every man was welcome into the brotherhood. Piracy offered men an unheard-of level of freedom and offered a chance for the oppressed of the late seventeenth century and early eighteenth century, black or white, to live a better life. As pirate captain Bartholomew Roberts said:

> In an honest service: there is thin Commons, low Wages, and hard Labour: in this, Plenty and Satiety, Pleasure and Ease, Liberty and Power; and who would not balance Creditor on this Side, when all the Hazard that is run for it, at worst, is only a sower Look or two at choaking. No, a merry Life and a short one, shall be my Motto.[6]

One of the earliest glimpses into pirate life was written by the pirate surgeon John Exquemelin, also known as Alexander Oliver Exquemelin, who presented in his book, *The Buccaneers of America*, a firsthand account of life among the pirates from the time he joined the buccaneers in 1669 in Tortuga until 1674. The term "buccaneer" generally refers to the privateers and pirates of the West Indies who plundered Spanish shipping in the Caribbean throughout the seventeenth century. The word originally applied to the groups of men, mainly French, who lived off the wild herds of cattle that roamed the northern regions of Hispaniola. They became known as *boucaniers* from their practice of roasting meat on a *boucan*, a type of barbecue similar to that used by the local Indians.[7] In addition to hunting cattle these rough lawless men attacked vessels. Buccaneer is often used interchangeably with pirate and privateer but that is not the original meaning of the word. Exquemelin described the pirates' highly organized democratic and civilized society on board ship and at the pirate islands of Tortuga and Hispaniola. The guarantees of civility and democracy were contained in the ship's articles that detailed all aspects of life onboard the ship. The articles were the foundation of the pirates' invented radical government.

Every man who became a pirate was required to take an oath and commit to the articles by signing his name, or making his mark, (usually an "X," if he was illiterate), in the steward's book.[8] The ship's articles were a contract that bound together men to work together for the good of the pirate society. The articles stated that members of the buccaneer commonwealth were expected to "be civil to one another, to aid their fellows in time of want, and to preserve the booty of dead pirates for their 'nearest relations' or their 'lawful heirs.'"[9] That last point—"to preserve the booty of dead pirates for their 'nearest relations' or their 'lawful heirs,'"— is very important because although a pirate ran his own commonwealth on the wooden decks of his ship and on pirate colonies, the articles make it clear that a pirate's community included family and loved ones and that provisions were to be made for them.

Exquemelin was the first source to mention the agreement between pirates to care for each other's relations in the event of their death. The agreement, called matelotage, is a partnership between two pirates to pool all their possessions.[10] "The pirates draw up a document, in some cases saying that the partner who lives longer shall have everything, [and] that the survivor is bound to give part to the dead man's friends or to his wife, if he was married."[11]

Pirates had created a complex, democratic world where the pirate ship was a business and the crewmembers were co-owners.[12] In 1984, the pirate ship *Whydah* was discovered off the coast of Wellfleet, Cape Cod and the ship's bell—considered the soul of the vessel because it regulates life at sea—was found near the crew's area, indicating that they ran the vessel. On warships and merchant vessels, the ship's bell would have been found near the captain's cabin. On the *Whydah*, as with other pirate vessels, every man was given a vote, but there was still a hierarchy with elected officers; it was a system that provided order in the pirate community, not chaos as the authorities claimed. The articles outlined the responsibilities of the captain and the quartermaster, who were usually selected "over a bowl of punch."[13] The captain was chosen for his superior knowledge of navigation and seamanship, as well as his ability to lead his men in battle or against troublemakers. A typical captain was either an officer from a West Indian privateer or a mate or boatswain from a merchant ship which had mutinied or been captured by pirates.[14] His tenure depended on maintaining the respect and goodwill of his men. If he lost their confidence, he could be outvoted and dismissed from his position.

The quartermaster was an able-bodied individual responsible for the discipline onboard. He had authority over the whole company, except when the pirate ship was called to action; during those times, the captain would maintain total command of the vessel. The quartermaster was "part mediator, part treasurer, and part keeper of the peace."[15] He was the captain's right-hand man. He was so influential he often became the captain of the vessel that was captured next. As the keeper of the booty, he was also one of the most important members of the crew.

Another feature of the ship's articles was to carefully articulate the distribution of booty. Some was allotted for compensation for the crew and some was set aside for special allowances for the men wounded in action. The special allowances were a sort of "health insurance" that the pirates provided because they cared so much about the well-being of their members they wanted to make sure they were fairly compensated for their pain and disability. On Exquemelin's ship, a pirate received 600 pieces of eight or six slaves for the loss of the right arm; 500 pieces of eight or five slaves for the left arm; 500

pieces of eight or five slaves for the right leg; 400 pieces of eight or four slaves for the left leg; 100 pieces of eight or one slave for the loss of an eye or a finger. And if a pirate suffered a severe internal injury, he would be compensated with 500 pieces of eight or five slaves.[16] After the salaries and the compensation for the wounded were paid out of the capital, the rest of the booty was divided by as many men who were on the ship, (boys received half a share), with the largest amounts going to those most vital to the operation of the pirate ship. For example, Exquemelin named the captain, the hunter (employed to get the food supply of meat, usually pork and turtle, for the ship), the surgeon and the carpenter as the most vital.[17]

This system of providing for others flies in the face of the many claims from colonial authorities that the pirates were uncivilized. Quite the contrary, they ran a sophisticated operation that took into account the needs of the pirate community.

Another of the inaccurate portrayals was that pirates were without values. But Exquemelin described in depth the values upheld by pirates. Honesty and loyalty were so important to the sustainability of the buccaneer commonwealth that it was determined that "[t]o prevent deceit, before the booty is distributed everyone has to swear an oath on the Bible that he has not kept for himself so much as the value of a sixpence ... And should any man be found to have made a false oath, he would be banished from the rovers, and never more be allowed in their company."[18]

The colonial authorities wanted the lawlessness on the high seas stopped and they were single-minded in their purpose of eradicating piracy by any means possible. Take for example a pirate trial. Once a pirate was caught and brought to trial his fate was sealed quickly. Often pirate trials lasted less than an hour and he was denied legal representation. Because many pirates were seamen with little or no education, many were unable to defend themselves or bring in witnesses to defend them because witnesses were very often out at sea. The king was considered the victim and the judge almost always did the Crown's bidding. After the trial, court transcripts were peddled on the street, keeping the image of pirates as ignorant criminals alive.

Political propaganda was one of the Crown's strongest and most enduring weapons. Of all the pirates who pillaged the seas over the last 3000 years, those of the Golden Age are the most famous, primarily because of the copious images found in eighteenth-century newspapers, court documents and books. For the most part, the propaganda portrayed them as intractable monsters, richly deserving of publicly humiliating and gruesome deaths. This image has persisted and inspired nineteenth-century novels and twentieth- and twenty-first century movies, television shows and pop-culture memorabilia. But as we now know, they are drawn from biased and inaccurate sources and as part of the colonial campaign to stamp out piracy. While of course some of the negative information we have about pirates is true, there is a wealth of detail about pirates in private correspondence and eye-witness testimony that hasn't made it into the public conscious-ness because portraying a pirate as a dastardly villain is far more interesting and gets more attention than portraying him as an or-dinary man.

Dubious Sources

Newspapers like the *Boston News-Letter* from July 3, 1704 re-ported the "wicked and vicious" lives of the pirates to readers who were both fascinated by and fearful of them. Politicians, literary men, ship owners and merchants gathered regularly at coffee-houses around London to read the latest news of the pirate's ac-tivities. What they didn't know was that the newspapers were often allied with the colonial authorities—the government either pub-lished the newspapers or the publishers were dependent on subsi-dies from the government or of the political parties, and felt pres-sure to slant the reporting toward their benefactors.[19] And lest we forget, the ocean was the pirates' workplace and since their crimes were carried out in remote places it was nearly impossible for any-one to know what really happened out there and report it prop-erly.[20] Word of pirate exploits was carried back to land by other ship captains or witnesses but it could take weeks, months, or even years for news to reach land in what amounted to a very long game of telephone, with details forgotten or exaggerated.

Another critical source about pirates is *A General History of the Robberies and Murders of the Most Notorious Pyrates*, written in 1724 by an anonymous source calling himself Captain Charles Johnson. Published in England, it was considered the first primary source book on pirates and it was an important and influential work because it was thought at the time to be—and many contemporary pirate enthusiasts and scholars still consider it—a comprehensive and, more importantly, *accurate* account of the pirates. A massive two-volume book, it details the lives and actions of contemporary pirates whom Captain Johnson described as "convict goal-birds or riotous persons, rotten before they are sent forth, and at best idel and only fit for the mines."[21] Johnson claimed he interviewed victims of pirates and some pirates themselves for his profiles of contemporary pirates. While these first-hand accounts are valuable, he also relied on source material that consisted of many of the same pamphlets, transcripts and contemporary newspapers that were published by the colonial authorities and it is from these tainted sources that Johnson created profiles of the most notorious pirates of the day. He posited that his subjects were so disgusting and dishonest they would return to piracy "like the Dog to the Vomit," after being pardoned by the King, as some of them were. Even the editor of *The General History*, Manuel Schonhorn, admitted in the Introduction that Johnson's accounts were fraught with problems; he embellished facts in Volume I and outright fictionalized part of Volume II. Although the *General History* is of debatable veracity, it is certainly an entertaining read and one can see why its popularity as a source has endured. However, it is a useful resource only in showing from where the popular opinion of pirates originated.

One example of the misleading information contained in the book is the chapter on Edward Teach, also known as Blackbeard, one of the most famous and feared pirates in history. Johnson described him with great drama as a monster and included a cartoonish illustration of a maniacal character with lit firecrackers in his ears.

His actions, according to Johnson, were even more monstrous. One night, while Blackbeard was drinking in his cabin with the

Illustration courtesy of the Library of Congress.

pilot of his ship, Israel Hands, and another man, he privately drew out a small pair of pistols and cocked them under the table. He blew out the candle and discharged them at his company. He shot Israel Hands through the knee, making him lame for the rest of his life. When asked why he did it, Blackbeard answered that if he did not kill a man every now and then, they would forget who he was. Johnson passed on as historical truth this wholly unsubstantiated story and it has endured uncorroborated for centuries. The truth was finally revealed in 2008 when Trent University historian Arne Bialuschewski discovered several forgotten accounts by captives and others about Blackbeard in archives of Jamaica. He reported that there was no evidence that Blackbeard ever used violence against anyone.[22] So numerous were the errors in Blackbeard's story that Johnson even got his name wrong. Recent research has also revealed that Blackbeard's name was not Teach at all, it was Thatch.

Unsurprisingly, British authorities often ignored the existence of the families of the pirates. Take the example of Captain Edward Low, who was reported to be so cruel and heartless there was nothing he would not do to his captives. One account has it that he slashed the lips off of a captain tied to the mast, had them boiled in the galley fire and made one of the crewmen of the captured ship eat them boiling hot.[23] Before Captain Low turned pirate, he was a ship-rigger in Boston where he met his wife, Eliza Marble, "an attractive young woman from a good family."[24] They were married in Boston and had two children. Sadly, Mrs. Low died shortly after giving birth to their second child, who died in infancy himself. Filled with sorrow over the loss of his wife and child and unable to take care of his young daughter, Edward Low left her in the care of a relative and went to sea, eventually turning pirate. Probably as a result of this tragic early life, Captain Low did not allow married men to join his crew. Philip Ashton, a fisherman captured in June 1722 by Captain Low off the coast of Nova Scotia and held captive for nine months, explained that Captain Low did not take married men on for a deeply personal reason: he knew the difficulty of being separated from family.[25] Captain Low felt this loss so intensely Ashton saw him openly weep at the mention of his wife and children. Clearly, it was easier for the colonial authorities to portray Captain Low as a violent monster than as a feeling man suffering profoundly from his personal losses.

As we are beginning to see, there is more to the pirate story than meets the eye and exaggerations and even outright lies have been absorbed into current popular culture and especially our understanding of the motives and inner lives of these men. These images ignore the private sphere of the pirates—the relationships they had among themselves and with their wives, families, and com-

munities back home. As will become clear in the chapters to follow, our picture of these very public men will be enriched and en-
hanced so that we finally see them with the wider lens they
deserve. We must consider their motives and fears and their desire
for a better life, albeit in many cases a short one.

In this book, I will delve into the inner lives of pirates, their
faiths, communal ties, and great loves. You'll hear about the wives,
families, and communities of four pirate captains from the Golden
Age who were active from 1695–1720. One of the most remarkable
things my research has revealed is the role women played in the
lives of pirates—a much larger one than has been acknowledged
in previous pirate literature. And you'll see that ethics and values
played a large role in their lives.

Though pirates were active up and down the eastern seaboard
of the United States and Caribbean, I've chosen to focus specifically on four pirates who operated in New England. This area was
a hub of pirate activity, and I chose these four pirates in particular
because they were all married, (except Samuel Bellamy, who had
an "intended"), all interacted with each other at some point or another, and because all of them were involved—in some cases,
quite actively involved—in the larger land-based community.
These men are Samuel Bellamy of Cape Cod, Massachusetts,
Paulsgrave Williams of Block Island, Rhode Island, William Kidd
of New York and Samuel Burgess of New York.

While I focus on these four men, my research included the lives
of eighty married pirates whose stories help craft a picture of the
wider world of pirates and the surprising sense of community
these men often shared, inspiring us to take another look at the
conventional image of pirate life.

As we have already seen, many of the original sources on pirate
life are not reliable. However, there is plenty of good information
if you know where to look. I have reconstructed the lives of the
four pirate captains from historical facts recorded in archived
criminal cases, depositions of captured pirates and witnesses,
memoirs of pirate captives, reports from colonial governors, Last
Wills and Testaments, land transactions, town clerk records, news-

papers, vital records (including birth, marriage and death certificates), dying words, and, in one instance, a prenuptial agreement. I also used correspondence that was found in a sea chest in Captain Samuel Burgess' pirate ship the *Margaret* when it was captured by a British privateer in 1699. Among the over two hundred documents in the sea chest were several letters from the pirates to their wives and families, and letters from wives and families to the pirates. These documents, called "prize papers" are in the National Archives in London. I also conducted interviews with experts of the *Whydah* pirates and benefited from their conversations and correspondence.

At the heart of this book is the idea that pirates have been misrepresented for centuries and portrayed as less than human. It is about how human values in the broadest and best sense extended into the community and the world of pirates in a way that has not be explored or expressed heretofore. The sea created a geographic boundary that separated the pirate from the traditional social institutions on land such as work, church and family, but pirate communities had a highly organized social structure designed to support and maintain their relationships on land while they were at sea. Pirates lived in their own civil society that cared for and protected their own as well as others. Quite often a pirate traveled thousands of miles to return the personal belongings and booty of a deceased pirate to his wife or relations. Pirates had a mail system that allowed them to keep in contact with family members back home. The pirates' "post office" was under a large rock with a hole in it located near where the ships came in on Ascension Island, a small remote island in the South Atlantic. New York merchant captains trading with the pirates in Madagascar dropped off and picked up the pirates' mail on Ascension Island on a regular basis. They also had an established program for retiring pirates—if a pirate paid 100 pieces of eight to the captain and supplied his own food and drink for the voyage, he could catch a ride on the next available ship from Madagascar to New York and return to society.

As we can see, the concept of human values was woven into the life of a pirate and this is an important component that has been overlooked in previous histories of pirate life. Captain Kidd, for example, sent his last piece of gold home to his wife Sarah before his execution. Before he was hanged at Execution Dock on the River Thames in London May 23, 1701, Captain Kidd told those around him to send his love to his wife and daughters back in New York City. He also said his greatest regret "was the thought of his wife's sorrow at his shameful death." And Captain Samuel Bellamy was an extraordinarily successful pirate, capturing over fifty ships in fourteen months and acquiring several tons of gold and silver. But he also exhibited such fairness to his captives that he was known as the "Pirate Prince."

Considering these men through the lens of their relationships to their wives, families, and communities brings out an under-standing of pirates that has not been previously considered and it shows that the pirates were not so-called "enemies of the human race." Rather, they were human beings, like us, who sought to live their lives under challenging circumstances as they attempted to meet their own needs but also those of their families and commu-nities.

CHAPTER 1

"Black Sam" and His Lady on the Shore

Captain Samuel Bellamy

Around midnight on Friday, April 26, 1717, the pirate ship *Whydah* crashed and sank off the coast of Cape Cod during a fierce storm. Captained by Samuel Bellamy, the one hundred foot, three-masted galley-style vessel was carrying treasure from over fifty ships. An estimated five tons of stolen gold and silver spilled on the ocean floor. One hundred and forty-six men were onboard; two survived.

For nearly three hundred years, the story of the *Whydah* (pronounced WHI-da) and her pirates was told in books, bars and as bedtime stories. Generations knew the story of the pirate captain called "Black Sam" from the west of England who perished with his treasure ship off Cape Cod. There were many versions to the story, some more embellished with intrigue and mystery than others, but the story of the shipwreck, the massive loss of life, the stash of treasure and a beautiful young woman named Maria Hallett is Cape Cod's most enduring legend. Few people believed there really was a pirate ship buried beneath the sand on one of Cape Cod's outer beaches, but every now and then something would appear that would lend credence to the story. A blackened silver coin with a very early date, a piece of eight, would wash ashore near where the wreck took place in Wellfleet, on the Atlantic side of the coast of Cape Cod. The lucky beachcomber would show it to a friend, record it in a family journal, or attach it as a charm to a bracelet. These stories were frequent enough to keep memories of the old wreck alive. An occasional sighting of a piece of shipwreck had the same effect. In the nineteenth century, Henry David Thoreau claimed to have seen the caboose (the stove) of the pirate ship at very low tide and wrote about it in his book *Cape Cod* in 1865. And more recently, in 1970, a piece of bone dated to the time of the shipwreck and believed to be from one of the pirates was found at the archaeological excavation site of Smith Tavern, a remote inn and favorite stopping place for mariners in the early eighteenth century, on Great Island in Eastham (present-day Wellfleet).[1]

Many people tried to find the *Whydah* over the course of three hundred years but the treacherous conditions on Cape Cod's outer shore where over 3000 ships have wrecked and the uncertainty of where the *Whydah* had settled in the shifting sand made it impossible for treasure hunters to find the elusive ship. However, in 1984, salvage expert and native Cape Codder Barry Clifford discovered the ship's bell under thirty feet of sand off the coast of Wellfleet. He used primary source documents from the early eighteenth century, including a map drawn by Captain Cyprian Southack, an experienced mariner and cartographer dispatched by the Crown to the *Whydah* wreck site to attempt to retrieve the ship's treasure. The bell's inscription "*The Whydah Gally 1716*" identified the ship, making it the first authentic pirate ship ever recovered.

With the discovery of the *Whydah*'s bell, the story of Samuel Bellamy and his pirates is no longer shrouded in myth. There were in fact pirates on Cape Cod in 1717, and the over 200,000 artifacts recovered from the wreck site on display at the Whydah Pirates' Museum in Yarmouth, Massachusetts prove these men were not imaginary figures. There is a size 5 men's shoe, a leg bone, a silk stocking, cutlery, pewter plates, homemade hand grenades, pistols, cannon, cannonballs, navigational instruments, medical supplies, game pieces, Akan gold jewelry from West Africa, gold and silver coins, and the shoulder blade of a pirate embedded in a teapot.[2] The artifacts give a fascinating glimpse of life aboard a pirate ship and each item helps piece together the story about Samuel Bellamy and the *Whydah* pirates.

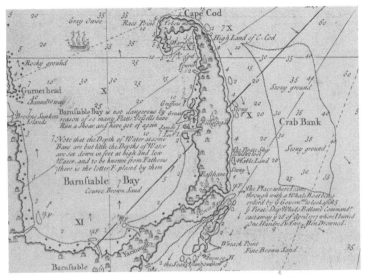

This map was used to find the *Whydah*. It was drawn by Captain Cyprian Southack in 1720 showing where the *Whydah* was lost and where 102 dead pirates were buried on Cape Cod, Massachusetts. Courtesy of the Library of Congress.

But there is one piece of the story that is not under plexiglass on a display table, or backlit against a cannon. That part of the story has to do with Samuel Bellamy, one of the most successful pirate captains in the Golden Age. His fearlessness established him as one of the most courageous pirates of the Caribbean. "Black Sam," as he was called because of his thick black hair, was in his mid-twenties and he had everything going for him — youth, success and even a title. Called "The Pirate Prince" because of his fair treatment of captives, Bellamy was considered royalty among the rich and famous (or infamous) of pirate society. Whydah Museum historian Kenneth J. Kinkor said the ship itself sank because of a beautiful young woman named Maria Hallett. "It could only have been because of Maria Hallett that

Captain Samuel Bellamy's pirate ship. Drawing courtesy of Steve Pope.

Bellamy made the sudden course change to Cape Cod," he said.[3] This would have put Bellamy at the center of one of the most devastating nor'easters in history.

Bellamy had intended to rendezvous in a few weeks time with other pirates at Damariscove Island in Maine but as he neared Cape Cod he made a detour. Bellamy was an experienced mariner; he knew the dangers of Cape Cod's outer shores. Legend has it that Maria Hallett lived in a hut in the dunes in Eastham. The *Whydah* crashed 500 feet from shore and very near her front door. Who is this woman who apparently charmed the "Pirate Prince?" She is critical to the *Whydah* story.

The best-known collection of Cape Cod lore about Maria Hallett and Bellamy is Elizabeth Reynard's *The Narrow Land*.[4] Recent research suggests that the legend of Maria Hallett, also known as Goody Hallett, may in fact be more truth than folk tale and is based on some historical events. According to the legend, Bellamy was visiting with friends at Smith Tavern on Great Island in Eastham in the spring of 1715 and decided to step outside to get some fresh air. Perhaps he needed a break from the smoke-filled bar or possibly to sober up from the free flowing rum toddies or "flips," frothy spiced ale drinks that were the tavern's specialty. In the distance, he heard a girl singing and followed the sound to the graveyard known as the Burying Acre where a young woman about fifteen years old with hair that "glistened like corn silk at suncoming" was standing under an apple blossom tree holding a lantern in one hand and apple blossoms in the other.[5] Maria Hallett looked at him with her enchanting hyacinth-colored eyes and it is said that Bellamy fell for her "with a crash that could be heard for miles."[6] Bellamy and Maria started spending time together and soon they were inseparable.

The townsfolk spoke of Maria's wild adventurous streak that challenged the principles of her parents' strict religious home. Her father, John Hallett, strongly objected to his daughter spending time with an unemployed English sailor ten years her senior. Determined to make something of himself so that he could have Maria, Bellamy sailed away and promised to return to Maria and "wed with a ring to the words of Rev. Mr. Treat, and in a sloop, laden with treasure, carry her back to the Spanish Indies, there to be made princess of a West Indian isle."[7]

About two months after Bellamy's departure from Cape Cod Maria discovered she was pregnant. Uncertain of where Bellamy was in the open seas of the Atlantic, Maria could only hope that he would return in a few months, as he promised. When it became evident she was pregnant, the townspeople banished her to "Lucifer Land," an appropriately named lonely and frightening hell.

The barren sandy area had only stubs of grass and was high on the cliffs of Eastham overlooking the Atlantic. Maria built a simple hut with her own hands to shield herself from the elements and waited for her baby to be born.

Bellamy did not return as soon as she thought he would. Sometime in the winter of 1716 Maria gave birth to a baby boy with black eyes and black hair. She delivered the baby herself, afraid to let anyone know. She hid the infant in a barn in Eastham and crept out to the barn regularly to feed him. Sadly, one day the baby choked on a piece of straw and died. Before she had time to bury him, the owner of the barn, a John Knowles, spied Maria holding her dead baby in her arms. Rumors spread and soon everyone believed she had murdered her baby to hide her shame. Justice Doane, the local authority, was alerted and Maria was taken to jail to await trial for the murder of her bastard child.

The jail keeper felt sorry for Maria and discretely left Maria's cell unlocked allowing her to escape back to Eastham where Maria returned to places that brought Bellamy's memory close—the hollow of the Burying Acre where the handsome Bellamy had made love to her, or to the outer coastline where she watched for Bellamy's ship. The locals found her, however, rearrested her and sent her back to jail. At least three times she escaped from jail and at least three times she was rearrested.[8]

The witch trials in Salem, Massachusetts were still fresh in people's minds. Even though they happened more than twenty years before, in 1692, Cape Cod was geographically close to Salem and Justice Doane and many of the town's people believed Maria was a witch. At night she cried and let out loud pained screams. It was uncertain if her outbursts were grief for her lost child, or the humiliation of her circumstances, but the townspeople assumed it must have been the devil that was visiting her—and that he must have been the one freeing her from jail time after time. How else could she escape the law and travel the distance from jail back to Eastham, a distance too far to walk, especially at night? Instead of sending her back to jail, and putting

her on trial for murder or witchcraft, the townspeople of Eastham stoned her out of town.

The loss of her baby, her time in jail, and public stoning left
Maria unmoored and without hope. Many believed only someone
connected with the devil could endure such pain. Maria made her
way back to her hut alone and outcast. She was a gifted weaver
whose beautiful creations were known and admired by the women
of the surrounding areas. Women brought their wool to Maria and
she traded her weavings for food and bread. Since Maria did not
want for food, the townspeople thought for sure she was a witch
and they called her "The Sea Witch of Billingsgate" (Billingsgate
was an area around Eastham). When the weather was foul and the
wind roiled the water some people said Maria was the cause of it;
she cursed the ocean stirring up waves and storms so that sailors—
or any sailor—would pay for her pains. Everyday, Maria was seen
walking on the bluffs or near the water's edge looking out towards
the ocean for her Bonnieman to return.

There is a Last Will and Testament in the records of Barnstable
County Probate Court in Barnstable, Massachusetts for a Mary Hallett from the eighteenth century.[9] She was born about 1693, making
her a young woman during the time Bellamy was known to be on
Cape Cod, and she lived in Eastham in 1715.[10] History records that
Bellamy lived in Eastham in 1715 and he let a room at Smith Tavern
on Great Island for several weeks or months before he sailed away
and turned pirate. Mary Hallett was the daughter of John Hallett,
Sr. and Mary Howes, from Yarmouth (a nearby town).[11] Mary was
the youngest of their six children and her older brother, John Hallett,
Jr., was a sailor married to Mehitable (Brown) Hallett whose parents
operated Smith Tavern. It is possible Mary lived with her brother
and sister-in-law and worked at the tavern, offering an opportunity
for Bellamy and Mary to have met there or in the surrounding areas.

The historic Mary Hallett was also related to John Knowles who
owned a barn in Eastham—he was her uncle. This lends credence
of the story where Maria hid in a barn owned by John Knowles.
The historic Mary Hallett died in 1751, childless and a spinster.[12]

Many believe Bellamy died in the shipwreck in 1717 and Mary could have stayed single and childless until her death.

It is also possible that Bellamy's lover was Mary's sister-in-law, Mehitable Hallett. Mehitable would have been called Goody Hallett—a nickname for Goodwife—because she was married and although she may not have been a faithful and good wife to her sailor husband, society still would have referred to her as Goody Hallett. With her parents' interest in Smith Tavern, it is possible Goody Hallett may have worked there doing day-to-day chores. It is of course possible that while her husband was away at sea, Bellamy and Goody Hallett had a relationship. Mehitable disappeared from the historical record in 1715 and was never heard from again. This coincides with the legend that Goody Hallett disappeared into the dunes in 1715 to await the birth of Bellamy's baby. History records that Mehitable's husband John Jr. remarried in 1716[13] so it is certain the marriage ended leaving open the possibility that she lived in the dunes waiting for Bellamy.

Another fact that meshes with the legend is that there actually was a Justice Doane in Eastham at the time; he was the justice of the peace and deputy sheriff. And locals claim Maria was imprisoned at the Barnstable jail, which is still standing and is listed on the National Register of Historic Places. The jail is a wooden saltbox built in 1690, twenty-five years before Mary was imprisoned there. It has six cells each the size of small horse stalls and a small opening the size of a fist allows light through the thick wooden doors. No bed, no chair, only a bucket on the dirt floor for the latrine. As a young woman staying there, Mary or Goody Hallett would have been subjected to a grim and frightening stay in a dark, dank cell.

There are enough strong similarities between the legend and historical events to reasonably believe there was a woman who influenced Bellamy's decision to return to Cape Cod. Ultimately, it does not really matter whether the woman was Maria or Mary or Goody Hallett—the woman in the legend could have been a composite of the three since legends often consist of several stories mixed together. Whoever the woman was, she was crucial to Bellamy's story and because of her we know so much more about pirates and

eighteenth-century Cape Cod culture—and we know that Samuel
Bellamy had someone special on shore waiting for him to return.

———————

Who was the real Samuel Bellamy? Biographical information
about his early years is scant but it is believed he was from the west
of England, from the neighboring village of Hittisleigh near Plymouth and was born March 18, 1689.[14] His parents were poor
farmers and Samuel was the youngest of Stephen and Elizabeth
(Pain) Bellamy's six children. A church record shows Samuel's
mother died soon after he was born.[15] When Bellamy was about
nine years old, the family moved to Plymouth, a hub for maritime
activity with sailors and traders working in the busy seaport. The
young Bellamy must have been influenced by his maritime sur-
roundings. When the War of Spanish Succession (1702–1713)
broke out, he was thirteen years old and by the end of that war
eleven years later, he was an experienced mariner able to navigate
a vessel, handle the sails and rigging, and use firearms and cannon.
Bellamy may have gained his seafaring skills working on a merchant vessel or a Royal Navy warship during the war.[16] And once
it ended, Bellamy, like thousands of sailors, was unemployed and
looking for work.

Bellamy first appears in historical records in 1715 in Provincetown, Massachusetts, the seaport town at the tip of Cape Cod. It
is presumed he left his native England to seek employment and to
visit relatives on Cape Cod. Centrally located near the hubs of
maritime trade in Boston, New York and Newport, Rhode Island,
Cape Cod was an ideal location for maritime opportunities. Bellamy let a room at Smith Tavern, an establishment owned by Israel
Cole, a man distantly related to Bellamy on his mother's side.[17]
Cole was a known smuggler and Smith Tavern served as a smugglers' den. The two-story clapboard structure was located on the
top of a sand dune in the woods above Cape Cod Bay and could
only be accessed by boat. Visitors to the tavern could look out the
diamond shaped windows and see who was coming and going, and
what was being loaded and unloaded.

Just a few months after Bellamy arrived on Cape Cod, a flotilla of eleven Spanish ships carrying more than fourteen million pesos from Havana, Cuba, to Spain wrecked off the coast of Florida during a huge gale on July 31, 1715. Millions of coins spilled on the ocean floor and word of the wreck created a flurry of activity for treasure hunters interested in a get-rich quick scheme. Just one casket of the precious metal would set one up for life very nicely. It is known that at Smith Tavern Bellamy had talked about going after the Spanish treasure. Amid all the discussion about the Spanish Plate Fleet, at least two people were convinced the Spanish treasure could be had—Bellamy and his friend, Paulsgrave Williams, a middle-aged, moderately successful goldsmith from Newport, Rhode Island. He was married with three children and he, too, had come to Cape Cod to visit relatives. The two began spending time together. There is no historical record of what transpired between Bellamy and Williams, but it is known that Williams put much of his personal wealth, as well as his future, into Bellamy's hands.[18]

During the next several weeks, the two acquired a boat, probably a small sloop, and assembled a crew of about a dozen men and set out for Florida in search of Spanish gold. But as we know, Bellamy and Williams were not the only men interested in the lost treasure. In scope, it had been compared to the California Gold Rush of 1849, and historians say it was *the* event that marked the peak of the Golden Age of Piracy.

Bellamy set sail for Florida in September 1715 and by the time Bellamy and Williams arrived at the wreck site off the eastern coast of Florida, near Vero Beach, the Spanish had so quickly and thoroughly swept the area, little was left for freeloaders.[19] Because the losses of the Spanish Plate Fleet nearly bankrupted Spain, who was already desperate for the gold and silver to pay off some of her wartime debt, the country was in dire financial straits. The king was even willing to have the treasure fleet, sailing as a convoy, attempt a risky crossing during hurricane season. With nothing to show for their venture, Bellamy and Williams must have wondered what to do next. For Bellamy, the idea of returning to Cape Cod a penniless sailor was out of the question. Going pirate may have been their only alternative.

Exactly when Bellamy and Williams turned pirate is unclear, but it is known that by February 1716, the two were actively plundering vessels. Merchant vessels sailing the trade routes of the Spanish Main were catnip for pirates. Their routes brought them through the Straits of Florida, or Crooked Island Passage in the Bahamas, through Windward Passage between Cuba and Hispaniola, or Mona Passage between Hispaniola and Puerto Rico.[20] So many pirate ships hunted them on the high seas the Governor of Bermuda wrote in 1717, "North and South America are infested with these rogues."[21] Historian Marcus Rediker estimated that between 1800–2400 pirates pillaged during the years 1716–1718.[22] Not surprisingly, the governor of Jamaica complained "... there was hardly a ship or vessel coming in or going out of the island that is not plundered."[23]

Bellamy and Williams made their first base of operations off the coast of Belize, in Central America. They traded their salvage boat for two fast and large sea going canoes called pirogues. The undecked, two-masted, flat-bottomed vessels were large enough to carry a few swivel guns, several dozen men, and were popular among pirates interested in quick-and-dirty raids in coastal waters. During this time Bellamy and Williams met John Julian, a Mosquito Indian from that area, who may have served as their guide. Julian turned out to be their first—and last—crewmember. He was the pilot of the *Whydah* and was one of the only two survivors of the shipwreck.

Success came early and easily for Bellamy and Williams. They were natural outlaws. They plundered several sizable ships in their first few months on the job, and their band of pirates was expanding in number and increasing in skill. Peter Cornelius Hoof, a thirty-three-year-old Swedish sailor volunteered to join the crew and brought great navigational know-how. For seventeen years, he had sailed on Dutch traders along the Spanish Main. Hoof's testimony at his trial in Boston nearly two years later would not be enough to convince colonial authorities he was not a pirate, and he met his demise at the gallows along with five other *Whydah* pirates. He was an important part of Bellamy's exploits for most of Bellamy's piratical career.

In April 1716, Bellamy, Williams and crew captured the *St. Marie*, a French merchant ship commanded by a Captain

L'Escoubes. The vessel held sixteen guns and forty crewmembers and turned out to be a smuggling vessel. Of that capture, Bellamy and Williams received about one third of the treasure that amounted to 28,500 Spanish pieces of eight.[24] It was around this time, in the spring of 1716, that Bellamy's career as a pirate took a turn. He met Benjamin Hornigold, a well-known pirate captain with years of experience robbing Spanish ships, and was formally instructed in the dark ways of piracy.

Bellamy and Williams met Hornigold near Cuba and joined his pirate band flotilla. Hornigold was the commander of the sloop *Marianne*, "a yellow-and-blue 8-gun sloop with worn, patched sails, manned by eighty seamen,"[25] and his Caribbean plundering partner, Captain Oliver Levasseur, also known as "La Buze," was master of the sloop *La Postillion*. Each sloop had a crew of eighty or ninety men and eight mounted guns. Hornigold operated out of New Providence, Bahamas, a popular pirate hideout. He taught piracy to capable and interested young men, and Bellamy became his new protégé. His most infamous student, Edward Thatch, also known as "Blackbeard," was a wild, flamboyant rogue who had been married fourteen times and captured approximately 140 merchant ships.[26] Hornigold was a former privateer for the king of England and maintained his loyalty to England, refusing to plunder English ships.

The pirates, now a larger group with Bellamy and Williams, continued an easy life of plundering, and in June 1716 they sailed to Samana Bay, on the coast of Cuba, to careen their vessels. Careening was an elaborate process that involved beaching the vessels, turning them on their sides, scraping the barnacles and other marine life off the hulls, and then covering the bottom area with a protective layer of tar. While the ships were being careened, a dispute arose among the pirates in the Hornigold flotilla having to do with Captain Hornigold and some of his English crews' refusal to plunder a British ship. Bellamy supported free-plunder, as did the rest of the crew. They demanded every merchant ship be considered fair game, regardless of nationality.

In accordance with the ship's articles, which state that crew can depose their captain by a show of hands, a vote was taken, and the crew of the *Marianne* voted to pursue all ships. Hornigold was deposed, and Samuel Bellamy was elected the new captain of the *Marianne*, a single deck New England sloop, built for speed and capable of holding forty tons of booty. Bellamy's quick rise to captain meant he was widely trusted by his fellow crewmembers. Bellamy allowed Benjamin Hornigold, the now ousted captain, to leave unharmed with a ship and his crew. This treatment towards an ousted captain is the reason Bellamy earned the nickname "The Pirate Prince." John Fletcher was elected quartermaster, William Main was appointed sailing master, and Jeremiah Burke the boatswain. John Brown and Hendrick Quintor, two of the six pirates later tried in Boston, were part of this crew, as was Paulsgrave Williams.[27] A captain whose vessel was later captured by Bellamy reported that there were 90 men on board and that "[t]he greatest part of the Pirates Crew are Natives of Great Britain and Ireland, the rest consisting of divers Nations and of 25 Negroes, taken out of a Guinea Ship."[28] The composition of Bellamy's crew reflected a typical pirate ship community—a multicultural, multiethnic community of sea robbers.

With his rise to captain, Bellamy would have created his own articles and the new crew would have signed them to promise to be true to the brotherhood. No copy of Captain Samuel Bellamy's articles has been found, but *Whydah* researchers reconstructed and paraphrased the articles based on written rules and unwritten attested customs common to pirate crews of the early eighteenth-century.[29] The articles also contain common practices followed by Samuel Bellamy and his crew. Captain Bellamy's articles are hardly the rules of a lawless band of uncivilized brutes.

The Articles of Captain Samuel Bellamy[30]

New members of a pirate crew were sworn to be true to both their shipmates, as well as to the Articles, and were "not to cheat the Company to the value of a piece of eight." New recruits were not considered part of the pirate ship's "Company," and so were not entitled to a share in any valuables taken, until they had signed the Articles.

1. Every Man who has signed these Articles is to have a Vote in all Matters of Importance.

2. The Captain and Officers of the Company are to be chosen by the Majority upon the commencement of a Voyage, or on such other Occasions as the Majority of the Company shall think fit.

3. Every Man shall obey Civil Command. The power of the Captain is supreme and unquestioned in time of Chase, or of Battle. He may beat, cut, or shoot any Man who dares deny his Command on such Occasions. In all other matters whatsoever, he is to be governed by the Will of the Company.

4. Every Man is to have Equal Right to the Provisions or liquors at any Time, and to use them at Pleasure unless Scarcity makes it necessary to vote a restriction for the Good of all.

5. Every Man is to be called fairly, in Turn, by the List of our Company kept by the Quarter-Master, on board of Prizes. Each Boarder on such occasions is to receive a Suit of clothes from the Prize. He who first sees a Sail, shall have the Best Pistol, or Small-Arm, from on board of her.

6. The Quarter-Master is to be the first man to go on board of any Prize: he is to separate for the Company's use what he thinks fit, and shall have Trust of the Common Stock until it be shared. He shall keep a Book showing each Man's Share, and each Man may draw from the Common stock against his Share upon request.

7. If any Man should Defraud the Company, or one another, to the Value of a Dollar, he shall be marooned or shall suffer what Punishment the Majority shall think fit.

8. Each Man is to keep his Musket, Pistols, and Cutlass clean and fit for Service upon inspection by the Quarter-Master.

9. No Woman or Boy is to be brought on board our Ship or to be meddled with without consent.

10. No married men are to be forced to serve our Company.

11. Good Quarters to be granted when called for. No prisoner is to be harmed after quarter has been granted unless he is voted punishment as a criminal by the Company.

12. Any Man who Deserts the Ship, Keeps any Secret from the Company, or who Deserts his Station in time of Battle, shall be punished by Death, Marooning, or Whipping, as the Majority shall think fit.

13. Not a word shall be Written by any of the Company unless it be Nailed Publickly to the Mast. None shall have any secret correspondence with any prisoner.

14. If any Man shall strike or abuse another of our Company, in any regard, he shall suffer such Punishment as the Majority shall think fit. Every Man's Quarrel is to be settled on Shore with Sword and Pistol under the direction of the Quartermaster.

15. All lights and candles must be put out before 8 o'clock at night. If any Man continues drinking after that hour, he must do it on the open deck. That Man who shall smoke Tobacco in the Hold without a Cap, or carry a lit Candle without a Lanthorn, shall receive Moses' Law (that is, 40 Stripes less one) on the bare Back.

16. No Man is to speak of breaking up our Way of Living till each of us has shared a thousand pounds.

17. If any Man should lose a Limb, or become a Cripple, he is to have 800 Dollars out of the Common Stock, and for lesser hurts, proportionately.

18. The Captain and Quarter-Master are to receive two shares of a Prize; the Sailing Master, Boatswain, Surgeon,

and Gunner, one Share and a half, and other Officers one
and a Quarter Shares.

After his overthrow by Bellamy, Hornigold parted company from
the flotilla, leaving with "26 hands in a prize sloop," and Bellamy was
left with about 90 men, most of them English.[31] Because Britain and
other imperial powers were anxious to eradicate piracy, the
governor-in-chief of the Bahamas, himself a former pirate, offered
a king's pardon to all pirates if they surrendered before September
5, 1718 and promised to end their plundering. Hornigold took the
king's pardon and in an ironic twist of fate, became a pirate hunter.
Bellamy and Williams never saw him again. Captain Levasseur of
the *La Postillion*, formerly with Hornigold, joined Bellamy and their
flotilla of two vessels continued their raids on merchant ships.

In the months ahead, Bellamy captured vessel after vessel in
rapid succession, gaining him a reputation as one of the most
courageous pirates of the Caribbean and one of the most successful
of the Golden Age.[32] He cruised and plundered, and was seemingly
everywhere at once. Only five other pirate captains in the period
1716–1726 captured more ships.[33] After battling a French armed
warship, primary source documents record him in October 1716,
north of the coast of Dominican Republic where he captured a
prison ship. He gained seven new men, including Simon Van Vorst,
of New York, and Thomas Baker, a Dutch tailor. In November
1716, he took the *Bonetta*, an inter-island trading vessel carrying
passengers and cargo from Antigua to St. Croix. From a deposition
filed by the ship's commander, Abijah Savage, with Governor Walter
Hamilton on November 30, 1716, we get a first hand account of his
pirate activity.[34] This document was generated because ship captures were so common by pirates that it was standard procedure for
the commander to immediately file a report at the nearest island
with the authorities. Captain Savage said Bellamy raised the Jolly
Roger—that pennant with the skull and cross-bones—as a sign of
his authority. He brought his vessel close to the *Bonetta* and he and
his men boarded. For fifteen days, from November 9th to November 24th, 1716, they ate their food and planned their next attack.
His men robbed passengers, stole cargo and, before releasing the

ship, the quartermaster asked the usual question: did anyone want to join the pirates? A young boy named John King wanted to join. A scene took place so dramatic the ship captain noted it in his deposition. The boy threatened bodily harm to his mother and "declared he would kill himself" if he was restrained from joining the pirates. Captain Savage said the boy was seen leaving with the pirates along with two others, and he was not forced.

After capturing and looting a string of ships, in December 1716, Bellamy and LaBuze spotted the *Pearl* and the *Sultana* off the coast of Guadeloupe. After looting the *Pearl* and forcing some of her crew to join up (which was only done when specific skills were needed), the remaining crew of the *Sultana* were put on the *Pearl* and dismissed.

Later in December 1716, Bellamy was spotted sixty miles from Saba by a cargo ship from Cork, Ireland, destined for Jamaica. The *St. Michael* was just east of her destination when Bellamy captured the vessel and robbed her cargo of prime Irish beef and other supplies. The beef would offer a welcome change from the usual mainstay of salted pork and turtle. When Bellamy asked who would like to go "on the account," there were no volunteers. Bellamy asked if there was a carpenter on board, and a Welshman, Thomas Davis, was conscripted. Three others were forced. Davis pleaded to be let go. Bellamy promised he would release him with the next captured vessel.

Laying over on a deserted island of Blanquilla, off the coast of Venezuela, the total pirate gang of 210 men held new elections to determine the captain and officers of the new vessel, the *Sultana*. Bellamy was again elected captain and made the *Sultana*, a galley, his flagship. Paulsgrave Williams was made captain of the sloop *Marianne*. This moving from ship to ship was part of the pirate cycle. Finding a better, faster, stronger ship was always their primary goal; there was no sentiment attached to their floating home. La Buze decided to leave the flotilla, and with his ninety men, went to raid shipping off the coast of Curaçao.

Bellamy continued to collect cargo and crew. A trap set by the British navy in St. Croix was meant to ambush Bellamy and five other pirate ships. Governor Walter Hamilton of Antigua, who had taken a deposition from Captain Abijah Savage of the *Bonetta,* had notified the British authorities. The British were fed up. Bellamy escaped the trap and gained well-seasoned hands from the band of pirates that escaped from two of the ships that evaded the ambush. Bellamy found them hidden on the island, eager to join crew and be among some of their own kind. Bellamy's vessel now brimmed with booty of all sorts, and crew of all nationalities and ethnic origins. One hundred and eighty men looked to him as their captain. The band of freebooters sailed westward, possibly along the north shore of Hispaniola, toward the heavily traveled (and lucrative) Windward Passage between Cuba and Haiti.[35] They may have stopped briefly at Rio de la Plata on the coast of what is now the Dominican Republic before going to see the activity in the Windward Passage.[36] This was February 1717. It did not take long for Bellamy to find his next prize.

When stalking a vessel, Bellamy often flew the flag of a European government as a ploy, until he assessed his target's strength. This process often took hours or even days. When he was on deck leading the charge to capture a merchant vessel he wore an elaborate red frock coat with lace cuffs and a silk kerchief around his neck. Unlike other pirate captains like William Kidd and Paulsgrave Williams, he did not wear a wig. He wore his black hair tied back in a ponytail fashioned with a ribbon.[37]

Bellamy saw on the horizon a three-masted galley with eighteen big guns. She was bound from Jamaica to London. When Bellamy decided to attack a vessel, he maneuvered within range and "raised the large black flag with a death's head and bones across," one of his crewmembers reported. For three days, the two galleys, the *Sultana* and the *Whydah* were matching speeds. Williams was in the sloop *Marianne,* a slower vessel, trying to stay up with the galleys. Finally, after a chase that took them from the Windward Passage to Long Island in the Bahamas, Bellamy closed in on the *Whydah.*[38]

Lawrence Prince, commander of the *Whydah,* was a veteran seaman with thirty years of experience and he was well versed in pirate ways. He knew pirates who took ships unopposed were generous in their treatment of captives. Captain Prince fired two cannon at Bellamy (just to say that he had fired) and then lowered his sails.[39] He and his crew of fifty men waited for the pirates to board his vessel. From the inscription on the ship's bell, "*The Whydah Gally 1716*," Bellamy knew the ship was relatively new. Below decks the pirates learned Captain Prince's profession—he was a slave trader. The ship was named for the trading port of Whydah on the Gold Coast of West Africa where slaves were captured, collected in factories and transported for sale to plantation owners in the West Indies by the Royal African Company. Whydah means "Paradise Bird," but when the ship was loaded with human cargo it was far from paradise for the 600 slaves below decks. They were positioned in a supine position shackled together in two places, in a space approximately thirty by one hundred feet. During the Middle Passage, those hellish months crossing the Atlantic, the captives were often confined and left to stew in their own excrement as the ship pitched and rolled. Nearly one-third of the captives died a horrible death during transport. The *Whydah* was a vessel of oppression.

There were no slaves on board, however, when Bellamy's men set foot on the wooden decks of the *Whydah*. Prince, a former Royal Navy officer, now a thirteen-year veteran at trading on the west coast of Africa, had already sold his cargo in Jamaica and was on his way home to London. He was taking a triangular route he had made only once, he said, from Africa, the Caribbean, and back to London.[40]

The pirates must have been surprised and thrilled when they searched the vessel; the compartments were stuffed with valuable cargo. A hundred elephant tusks were stacked like logs of wood, bags of lapis-blue indigo dye filled other parts of the hold, and slabs of quinine bark, a popular medicinal substance, were fastened tightly together for efficient storage. Other areas had large sacks of sugar and casks of molasses.[41] Further inspection found a pirate's dream—sacks and sacks of gold and silver. Thirty-four-year-old veteran pirate Peter Hoof testified at his trial in Boston that locked in chests between the decks was bags of money: "20,000 or 30,000 pounds [sterling] was put up in bags, fifty pounds [weight] to every man's share, there being 180 men on board."[42] In addition to the sacks of doubloons and pieces of eight, there were bags of gold dust, bars of silver and gold, and Akan gold jewelry from West Africa. It was rumored that a small casket of East

Indian jewels was aboard, with a ruby the size of a hen's egg.[43] Inspecting the booty, Bellamy must have felt satisfied they had enough because he ordered a northern course towards the Virginia coast. Bellamy knew he had a fine vessel. He had chased her for three days and it is estimated she may have sailed at a speed of up to thirteen knots—quite fast for an eighteenth century vessel. She was heavily armed with eighteen cannon that fired cannon balls ranging from three to six pounds, and had a few swivel cannons that were useful for firing at opposing ships.

Bellamy told Captain Prince he was not only taking his cargo, he was also taking his ship. He anchored the *Whydah* off Crooked Island and redistributed the booty. The cargo from the *Sultana* was loaded on the *Whydah*. The *Whydah* was then overhauled to be a pirate ship. Over ten cannons taken from previous plunders were mounted on the bulwarks giving the *Whydah* twenty-eight guns, a large number for a vessel one hundred feet long and three hundred tons. They also loaded another dozen cannons, and picked up as many as ten new pirates from Prince's fifty-man crew: six who volunteered, and three who were forced.[44] The pirates held another vote for the officers of their new ship. Bellamy was elected captain of the *Whydah*. He made it his flagship. Richard Noland, a veteran of the Hornigold band, replaced John Fletcher as quartermaster. John Lambert became sailing master and Jeremiah Burke, boatswain. Paulsgrave Williams was re-elected captain of the *Marianne*.

Bellamy gave Captain Prince the *Sultana*, the remaining crew, and a small amount of supplies to make it to port. Bellamy also gave the former *Whydah* captain twenty pounds sterling as a parting gesture.[45] Thomas Davis, the Welch carpenter forced from the *St. Michael*, petitioned Bellamy for release, hoping to leave with Prince and his remaining crew. Bellamy was willing to let him go, but when the *Whydah* crew learned of Bellamy's agreement, the issue was put to a vote. By majority vote, the crew reversed Bellamy and reacted violently saying they would first shoot him or whip him to death at the mast.[46] It is possible the crew did not want to release Davis for fear he would run to the authorities and turn them in.

One must wonder if Bellamy paused to delight in the progress he had made in his new career in so short a period of time. His once small band of a dozen treasure hunters that left Cape Cod in search of Spanish treasure now numbered one hundred and eighty pirates. With each plunder he gained cargo, crew, or both. He was now an independent power and a predatory force to be reckoned with. The addition of his companion and partner, Paulsgrave Williams on the *Marianne* made their small flotilla a sort of mercenary navy. This process of going from a small band to a larger independent group is a key component of the piracy cycle.

In every nook and cranny of the *Whydah*, valuable cargo swayed to the rise and fall of the waves. The load of booty was said to be one of the biggest hauls made by pirates in the Caribbean. Still there was room for more loot and Bellamy steered his new vessel southward to continue plundering the Caribbean Basin where more unsuspecting vessels would be his prize. Near Haiti, off Petit Goave, the pirates took a Jamaican vessel chartered by French merchants to sail to Rochelle, France. The frigate *Tanner* was carrying a cargo of sugar, indigo, and about 5,000 livres in French currency. Quickly the silver currency was added to the collection in the *Whydah* hold.[47]

The pirate flotilla made an easy and uneventful voyage north from Haiti. Uneventful, because the British guard ships had not yet left their winter posts in the Caribbean for their New England posts in the spring, where they tried to intercept pirate ships preying on merchant vessels bound to and from England and the Leeward Islands. This left the coast clear for the pirate captains, Bellamy and Williams, to plunder at will. In the meantime, until they reached the North American coast, and until they found a vessel to prey upon, the pirates passed the time with the usual seafaring activities. They cleaned their muskets and pistols, and practiced target shooting.[48] They played checkers, backgammon and a variety of card games.[49] Some of their gaming pieces were even found at the wreck site.

Just imagine these men, dressed in sturdy clothing coated in tar to resist foul weather. Short and strong in stature, they averaged about five feet, two inches tall. Afflicted by smallpox and ringworms, tanned and leathery from the sun, and with a rolling gait that developed after months on a ship's constantly moving deck, they were a motley barefoot crew. Although they did not share a common language, or a common country, they hoisted sails and climbed rigging for one purpose and one purpose only—the one nation they could all call their own, the wooden deck below their feet. They were a floating democracy, joined by the seas. They cursed freely (especially if there was plenty of rum), and their manner of speaking was all their own. They were a unique community in which the black flag with a skull and bones across was their symbol of solidarity for all those who shared in this radical social experiment. The *Whydah's* black flag, flying boldly atop a tall wooden mast, was a symbol of their commonwealth.

One hundred and twenty miles from South Carolina, Bellamy plundered a Boston sloop captained by Simon Beer. Bellamy, after detaining Beer for two hours and removing his cargo, offered to release Beer, his crew and his ship. Bellamy's crew protested, fearing he may turn them in to the authorities. The crew voted to sink his boat and keep him prisoner on William's sloop, the *Marianne*. Bellamy is reported to have said to him, "D—my Bl—d ... I am sorry they won't let you have your Sloop again, for I scorn to do any one a Mischief, when it is not for my Advantage."[50] Beer and his crew were transferred to the *Marianne*, and his Boston sloop was sunk.

Soon after Beer's capture, the flotilla was separated by a storm that seriously damaged the *Whydah's* mainmast and threatened to sink her.[51] It is possible the damage made fragile the *Whydah's* structure, making her more vulnerable to the later fateful storm. Primary source documents show that the pirates were aware of the storm and made plans of where to meet, if separated. It was early spring now, about March 1717. The pirates planned to cruise for ten days off Delaware Bay after raiding off the capes of Virginia, then spend another ten days targeting vessels bound for the West Indies in the Philadelphia and New York area. Ultimately, the flotilla would reunite at Damariscove Island in Maine.

Depositions show the *Whydah* continued to plunder in rapid fashion. In one day, April 7, 1717, Bellamy captured three vessels. At about 8:00 a.m. they took the merchant ship *Agnes* bound for

Virginia from Bermuda. The vessel was taken fifteen miles off Cape Charles, Virginia. Rum, sugar, molasses, and European goods were their prize from Captain Tarbett's cargo hold. The ship and the crew were released, giving Bellamy time a little later in the day to go after the *Anne*, a one-hundred-ton galley from Glasgow, Scotland, mastered by Alexander Montgomery. Bellamy thought they should add this as an auxiliary vessel to the fleet, and he placed quartermaster Richard Noland in charge of it. Bellamy then captured the *Endeavor*, a pink—a slow-sailing bulk cargo hauler—from Brighthelmstone, England.[52] John Scott captained the *Endeavor*. Bellamy released the ship and crew after five days.

Bellamy's success in the area was so widespread he essentially shut down the commerce of the Chesapeake Bay, one colonial official complained.[53] Governor Spotswood of Virginia was greatly disturbed by the destruction the pirates were doing to North American trade. With the advice of the Council of Virginia he dispatched a letter to the governors of New York and New England to warn them of Bellamy and Williams and encouraged them to order out their guard ships to intercept the pirates.[54]

Governor Spotswood was desperate for reinforcements to protect the Chesapeake Bay area from Bellamy and all pirates. He pointed out to the Lord Commissioners for Trade and Plantations, and the Secretary of State, the need for support to either dislodge the pirates by force or the offer of pardon. Of the alternatives, he urged offering pirates the king's pardon, a proclamation known as "Acts of Grace," if they turned themselves in and promised not to return to their evil ways. Skeptically, he noted, "pirates would accept pardons, but few would reform, and most would quickly return to their old ways."[55]

For the next two weeks, the *Whydah* all but disappeared. History goes silent from the period April 7, 1717, to the fateful day, April 26, 1717. Captain Charles Johnson in *A General History of the Pyrates* records that during that period Bellamy went to a sheltered beach in Maine where he built a fort and careened the *Whydah's* hull. But his account of Bellamy's movements at that time does not ring true with the *Whydah* historian who believes there would not have been enough time for Bellamy to do all Captain Johnson claimed he did and get back to the Cape Cod area where history next records him.[56] Wherever Bellamy was, the waters of the Chesapeake were given a welcome break from his predatory attacks during this time.

The next time history records Bellamy's whereabouts is April 26, 1717. For fourteen months Bellamy had plundered the Caribbean Sea. Now he continued to prey on ships as they rode the southwestern wind towards Cape Cod. About nine in the morning, a Dublin merchant ship, the *Mary Anne*, (not to be confused with Paulsgrave Williams's ship the *Marianne*), came into view when the *Whydah* was halfway between Nantucket shoals and St. George's banks. The *Whydah* approached the ship that had just touched at Boston and was bound for New York.[57] Bellamy brought his ship alongside and ordered the *Mary Anne* to strike his colors. Captain Andrew Crumpstey immediately did as he was told, including spilling the wind from the *Mary Anne's* sails to stop the ship in the water. Bellamy hoisted a rowboat over the side and sent seven pirates armed with muskets, pistols and cutlasses to man his new prize. Thomas Baker, the former tailor from Holland, was in charge of the boarding party. Second in command was a tough-talking Jamaican named John Brown who was armed with pistols and a sword. Another pirate was John Shuan, a twenty-four-year-old Frenchman who was unarmed, and Thomas South, a forced man from a ship taken earlier, who made it clear to the captured crew he was not a pirate, and did not want to be one.

The captain of the *Mary Anne*, and five of his crew, was ordered to go aboard the *Whydah* with his ship's papers. Three members of the *Mary Anne* remained on the vessel: the mate, Thomas Fitzgerald, and two seamen, Alexander Mackconachy and James Dunavan.[58] The manifest from the *Mary Anne* revealed that the vessel held more than seven thousand gallons of Madeira wine. In the last twelve months, Bellamy had captured a ship about every two weeks: his loot was profitable but not potable, and soon Bellamy sent more men to the *Mary Anne* to retrieve at least two barrels of wine for his crew.

In a small boat, the *Whydah* pirates rowed to the nearby vessel. Onboard, the men found it difficult to get at the barrels of wine stored below decks because large coils of rope blocked the casks. The pirates raided Captain Crumpstey's cabin and helped themselves to his personal stock of wine, returning to the *Whydah* with several of the Captain's bottles. The pirates also brought back some clothing needed by the men from the *Mary Anne*.[59] Soon after, the rowboat was hoisted aboard the *Whydah* and Bellamy ordered the *Mary Anne* to follow him on a north-by-northwest course toward Cape Cod.

It was late April; the wind was coming off the land from the southwest carrying with it the sweet smell of spring. After over a year at sea, the pirates would touch land again soon. The small fleet followed the course until about four o'clock in the afternoon until they came upon thick fog in an area near to what is now Chatham, Cape Cod. *Whydah* researchers believe that most of the crew was on deck since the ship was so heavily laden with cargo from their season of successful raiding. Twenty-eight cannon were known to be on her, as well as elephant tusks, sugar, molasses, rum, cloth, quinine bark, indigo, and tons of dry goods that could easily be sold in the colonies and the precious gold and silver estimated to weigh about five tons (180 sacks of coins, each sack weighing fifty pounds)[60] stored in chests between the decks. With all that cargo, the *Whydah* would have sat low in the water, and it would not have taken much in the way of bad weather to jeopardize the sailing vessel.

Bellamy ordered his crew to loosen the sails to let the wind out, allowing the *Whydah* to remain still in the water until the weather's intentions became evident. Not having a local pilot to guide the way, it was too dangerous to risk proceeding through such thick fog. Within thirty minutes, a small sloop named the *Fisher* emerged through the fog. Captain Bellamy shouted to the captain, Robert Ingols, and learned he was a coastal trader who plied these waters many times. Ingols was from Virginia heading to Boston and his vessel was loaded with tobacco and hides.[61] Bellamy ordered one of his crew, David Turner, to send a four-man crew to capture the *Fisher*.[62] It was Bellamy's intention to use Robert Ingols and his mate as pilots to navigate the treacherous waters; they would be the eyes to steer this small flotilla to safety.

The weather worsened at about 5 o'clock. Quartermaster Richard Noland brought the *Anne* under the *Whydah*'s stern and hailed Captain Bellamy, informing him that land had been spotted through the mist. A change of direction was quickly ordered, the vessels were to take a northerly course to skirt the land rather than a northeastern course to get away from it.[63] *Whydah* researchers believe this is another indication that Bellamy intended to stop at Cape Cod and he was underestimating the potential force of the gathering storm.

Fog increased as the night came on and Bellamy ordered all four vessels to hang lanterns from the yardarms so they would not lose each other in the darkness.[64] The *Anne* and *Mary Anne* were in front followed by the *Whydah*, and then the tiny *Fisher*.[65] Soon the *Mary Anne*, a slow-moving vessel, fell out of formation. Bellamy hailed John Brown of the *Mary Anne* and told the pirates to make more haste. John Brown shouted that he would "sail until she carries her masts away."[66] John Brown's words may have been slurred, for he, like all the pirates on board the *Mary Anne*, were sloppy drunk from helping himself to the vessel's cargo of Madeira wine. It was reported that inside the vessel's close quarters, things got testy. At one point, running low on wine, Van Vorst, the pirate, told one of the crewmen he would 'break his neck' if he could not find more alcohol. The same crewman, Alexander Mackconachy, was then threatened by Thomas Baker, who, according to later legal depositions, growled that he would no more shoot Mackconachy through the head than he would a dog and that he should never go on shore to tell his story about his time with the pirates.[67] Whether anyone would survive was a question at that point. The weather was growing worse and the *Mary Anne* was taking on so much water through its leaky hull, the crew was forced to pump hard to keep afloat. The pirates are reported to have damned the vessel and wished they had never seen her.[68]

One can only speculate what went through the mind of Samuel Bellamy as the weather worsened. If he had known there was a strong storm coming, he may have risked it anyway because it was late April, past the usual New England storm season, and he was determined to reach his destination with his ship loaded with precious cargo. He had every reason to believe this storm would pass quickly, since earlier in the day it had been warm, with the wind out of the southwest off the land. Just a few hours before it had promised spring, how could a storm so fierce brew so quickly? Without modern-day technology showing changing weather patterns, it would have been impossible for the pirate captain to know he was sailing into a nor'easter. Within a very short period of time, high winds, heavy rain, and severe lightning would torment the North Atlantic by Cape Cod.

As the wind shifted, the waves of the North Atlantic swelled. White caps and cold sea spray would have been what the pirates saw, felt, and tasted. It grew more menacing as the night wore on, and by ten o'clock in the evening the weather worsened. The wind blew from the east, lightning pierced the sky, and it rained hard. Through the thick weather the vessels lost sight of each other.[69] If only this front had come earlier in the day, the pirates could have altered their direction away from Cape Cod, which was so infamous for its multitude of shipwrecks. But the pirates were trapped now and they had only their nautical skills and fearlessness to apply to this deadly situation.

The small flotilla was now separated by fog and darkness. The *Mary Anne* and the *Fisher* had lost sight of the *Whydah*, and the *Fisher* was blindly following the *Mary Anne*.[70] The seamen could not see the breakers until they were among them, but they dropped anchor trying to hold off their vessel from running aground on the shore. All hands tried to trim the headsail but the *Mary Anne* ran ashore before they could do it.[71] Thomas Baker, sober enough to think of protecting the vessel from catastrophe, grabbed an axe and quickly chopped down the foremast and mizzenmast to keep the vessel from tipping over when she hit the shore.[72]

The crew of the *Mary Anne*, fearful of getting caught by the authorities, took refuge in the lower deck of the vessel. "For God's sake let us go down into the Hould and Die together," one pirate said.[73] They asked one of the forced crewman, nineteen-year-old Thomas Fitzgerald, first mate to Captain Andrew Crumpstey, to read to them by candlelight from the Church of England's *Book of Common Prayer*, a religious tome that calls on sinners to repent. We know that Fitzgerald read to them for about an hour.[74]

When dawn broke that Saturday morning, the *Mary Anne* was still intact and on the shore. They were so close that the seven pirates and three sailors could jump directly onto land.[75] They had washed ashore on a small island called Pochet Island near Eastham,

Cape Cod. Alexander Mackconachy, the *Mary Anne's* fifty-five-year-old cook, went about his job and served breakfast to the men. He brought out a chest of sweetmeats (sugared fruits) from the cargo of the vessel, and more of that Madeira wine to wash it down.

The *Fisher* and the *Anne*, commanded by veteran pirate Richard Noland, were also successful in surviving the storm. The vessels suffered only moderate damage as they rode out the storm anchored north of the *Whydah* wreck site.[76] The following morning, the *Fisher* was looted and its prize crew, captives, and cargo were brought aboard the *Anne*.[77] The *Fisher's* hatches were opened and the vessel was abandoned at sea as the *Anne* made for Maine to rendezvous with the *Whydah*, which they assumed had survived the storm since it was nowhere in sight. When Bellamy failed to arrive, the pirates aboard the *Anne* continued looting a handful of fishing vessels along Cape Ann and the Maine coast on their way to the Bahamas.[78] Noland reconnected with his former commander, Benjamin Hornigold, and later accepted the king's pardon with Hornigold in 1718. He turned more or less respectable, and testified at pirate trials as a character witness.[79]

The tipsy crew of the *Mary Anne* noticed that the three masts of the *Whydah* were not visible on the horizon. It turned out Bellamy had not been as fortunate as his consorts. He had had no choice but to try to ride out the storm. Unlike some other vessels, galley-style vessels handle poorly in high winds, and the rising gale coming from the northeast made it virtually impossible for the ship to tack out to sea to avoid the shore.[80] A northerly approach was his only hope of buying time until the storm weakened. But the powerful winds, estimated to be about seventy miles per hour, made it impossible to stay on a northerly course. The *Whydah* was pushed west towards breakers. Thomas Davis, one of the two sole survivors, testified in Admiralty Court in Boston that Bellamy ordered the main anchor dropped as a measure to turn the ship around so that the *Whydah* could face the waves and avoid capsizing.

While the ship continued to turn, she hit a sandbar. The stern had run aground and the ship could turn no more. Legend has it that Bellamy swore as the *Whydah* struck the sand bar that he would see Maria Hallett if he had to sail his vessel over the dunes to her door.[81] More water swept the decks and within fifteen minutes of running aground, the mainmast snapped off and floated free. Nothing was left to hold the *Whydah* upright; she began to turn on her side. As she did, cannons and goods stored below came crashing through the decks crushing anyone in the way. Those who were able to get off the ship and knew how to swim did so, but very few sailors knew how to swim in the eighteenth century, and even if they could, the water was a frigid forty degrees—so cold few could make it 500 feet to the shore. The two survivors were Thomas Davis, the Welsh carpenter from the *St. Michael* who had been taken earlier, and the veteran pirate John Julian, the Cape Cod Indian, pilot of the *Whydah*. They were washed ashore with the debris and managed to climb to the "tableland," the flat area above the shoreline. The wreckage of the ship spread four miles and 102 dead pirates washed ashore so mangled by the sea and the tremendous impact of the shipwreck it was impossible to identify any of them.

What happened to "Black Sam" Bellamy? Many believe the twenty-eight-year-old pirate captain perished in the shipwreck with his crew, their possessions and their vast amounts of treasure. The trail of historical documents about his piratical exploits end with the shipwreck. But legend has it that he survived. One version says that a man's voice was heard in Goody Hallett's hut soon after the shipwreck; that Bellamy had come for her and they escaped together. Locals confirmed that after the shipwreck Goody Hallett was not seen again in her hut trading her weaving for food or walking on the bluffs. Elizabeth Reynard wrote that in the autumn of 1717, several months after the shipwreck, a tall stranger appeared and stopped in at Smith Tavern. His hair was black with a streak of white in front. His eyes were dark and there was a deep scar on his forehead. He wore a high button coat with lace at his wrists and he had plenty of money to spend. But his mind was unclear and he was lost in his thoughts. He look bewildered and occasionally moved his hands as if he was steering the wheel of a ship. He died in the summer of 1720 in the apple tree hollow by the Burying

Acre. He went there often as if he was waiting for someone. His body was carried to Smith Tavern and a belt of gold was found on his body. The men who saw him said that he had the face of a brave and young man.[82]

What really happened to "Black Sam" Bellamy is impossible to know, but one thing is certain—"Black Sam" was a far more complicated pirate than history has led us to believe. He was not only a courageous young upstart with a natural talent for deep-sea marauding, he was an ordinary man who desired (at least for some time), to interrupt his life at sea, step out of the wooden world of his pirate ship, and come ashore to be with a beautiful young woman. It was a very un-pirate thing to do.

CHAPTER 2

Deep Roots and Family Ties

Captain Paulsgrave Williams

aptain Cyprian Southack's map marked the spot where the treasure ship *Whydah* crashed and where 102 dead pirates washed ashore on Cape Cod. In a fateful move, one pirate who was not near the disaster was Paulsgrave Williams, "Black Sam" Bellamy's piratical partner. Ten days before the shipwreck, in a pre-arranged agreement with Bellamy, Williams veered away from the *Whydah* and he and his crew of about forty men sailed the *Marianne* into Block Island's secluded harbor. He was visiting his aged mother and three sisters, Mary, Elizabeth and Catherine, at the family home on Block Island. From shore his sloop would have been easy to spot with its yellow and blue hull, old patched sails and splintered mast. His visit home was brief, perhaps a few hours or a day or two because he and Bellamy planned to rendezvous at Damariscove Island in Maine to careen their vessels.[1] Scrubbing the barnacles and sea worms off the hulls would be good for business; it would increase their speed and maneuverability so that future ship captures would be smooth, quick surprise attacks. His detour was uncannily timed; the stopover spared him from the ruin with his shipmates on Cape Cod. It also shifted the focus away from the young charismatic Bellamy to the middle-aged jeweler turned pirate captain who, for the first time in his piratical career, was separated from his comrade and can be seen as a stand-alone eighteenth-century pirate captain.

Williams interrupted the plundering attacks on the high seas to return to his land-based underworld on a remote island in the Atlantic. Block Island is thirteen miles from the coast of Rhode Island, on the east end of the Long Island Sound, and is part of the colony that was such a hotbed of political, economic and social activity it was nicknamed "Rogue's Island." The inhabitants of Rhode Island were independent and feisty. With Block Island so close to its southern coast, yet far enough away to establish a world of its own—with its own militia, economy and system of governance—it was a pirate nest, a small one compared to the pirate nest of New Providence in the Bahamas, but nonetheless it had a reputation as a "free port to illegal traders and pyrates from all places."[2] Its remote location and secluded deep-water harbor made it an ideal place to unload illegal cargo. It is highly probable that Williams returned home to unload some stolen goods and possibly make contact with a fencing operation.[3]

Unbeknownst to Williams, his detour to Block Island did much more than he intended: it shed light on Block Island as this pirate's safe house, and his visit with his family put a human face on the inhuman pirate persona widely advertised by the colonial authorities. Williams' stopover at Block Island was common knowledge among the pirates, but it was a carefully guarded secret from the public, as all pirate activities were. The surprising news that even a pirate has a mother and sisters was disclosed quite by accident in a deposition given by one of Williams' crewmembers, Jeremiah Higgins, who ran into trouble with the law. Higgins casually mentioned in one short sentence that Williams detoured to Block Island to see his mother and sisters and while Williams went ashore to see his family he stayed onboard the *Marianne*.[4]

It is very rare for modern historians to know this much about the family of an eighteenth-century pirate because pirates usually didn't live long enough to grow old and write about their origins. And others were careful to conceal their background so that they could anonymously slip back into society with their ill-gotten loot. Williams's pause from his piratical activities allowed us to learn more about his life, not as a pirate who belongs to the "lowest rungs of society," but as a family man. The Block Island Town Record Book, genealogical records, Last Will and Testaments, land evidences and a prenuptial agreement all show that he came from a very successful landowning family, many members of which were highly educated and deeply involved in the political and economic events of the seventeenth and early eighteenth centuries in Massachusetts, Rhode Island, and especially Block Island where he had deep roots. In his family there were doctors (men and women), merchants, civil servants and even an appointed official. His father, John Williams, was the Attorney General of Rhode Island. Williams's detour revealed a treasure trove of information that would never have been known if he had followed the posse of pirates to Cape Cod.

It was Saturday, April 17, 1717, and Williams had been a pirate for two years. He was a hardened criminal now, his skills were finely tuned as a maritime predator and he had an impressive record to prove it: he and Bellamy had captured over fifty ships. Of medium build with a dark brown complexion, even in the tropical sun and damp sea air Williams chose to wear the fashion of the day—a peruke (a wig).[5] Williams' wig was a sign of the forty-one-year-old pirate captain's interest in being part of respected society, not an outsider.

On Block Island Williams would have known almost everyone; his family had lived on the island for over fifty years. He would not have needed to "sign in" when he arrived in New Shoreham, the island's main town, as every visitor did, or pay a £5 fine.[6] That rule was for outsiders and Williams was no outsider; he wore a wig to prove it and as an insider he could "help" his fellow Block Islanders who were so short of cash from the British trade restrictions they bartered pork, beef, wheat, barley, butter, tallow and cheese as legal tender.[7] His stolen goods and gold and silver coins would be very appreciated and quickly the booty would filter through Block Island's economy and the economies of the larger environs, reviving it like a good drink of water.

A son going home to see his mother in his pirate ship certainly doesn't fit the image we usually think of when we think of the pirate, especially with a ship that looked like his. He had been sailing the stolen French merchant ship for more than a year and still he did not convert it, like some pirates did, to a menacing "enemy of the human race" vessel, as they called pirate ships. It did not have the typical pitch black colored hull, crisp strong sails and a skull and cross bones flag flying high over the main mast. Instead, he kept the paint, the sails and the rather wimpy name, the *Marianne*. All that mattered, of course, was the stolen loot hidden below the wooden decks, out of sight of the authorities, and conveniently available to unload at a desired location. His mother's home may have been the desired location. Or perhaps his sisters' homes— Mary and Elizabeth lived on Block Island with their husbands and children. The island was small, just seven miles long and three and a half miles wide, so it would have been easy for Williams to reach them. Catherine, too, lived nearby at Cowneck (Sands Point), Long Island with her husband and growing family.[8]

The women in the Williams family were no strangers to dangerous illegal activity. Eighteen years ago, in 1699, Williams's older sister, Mary, and her husband, Edward Sands, were close friends of the notorious pirate Captain William Kidd and his wife, Sarah. They were close enough that Sarah Kidd stayed at the Sands' home on Block Island when Kidd was on the run from the law. The Sands went on board Captain Kidd's sloop when he was moored off of Block Island for a brief time, and Mary, as Sarah's companion, was onboard Captain Kidd's sloop when he sailed from Block Island to Gardiner's Island, a remote island in Long Island Sound, and buried some of his stolen treasure. The couple was heavily implicated as possible criminal accessories in the events surrounding the manhunt throughout New England for Captain Kidd. Williams's younger sister, Elizabeth, and her husband, Thomas Paine, (possibly the nephew of Captain Thomas Paine who was involved in the Captain Kidd affair), were also implicated in helping Captain Kidd.[9]

It is also possible that Williams gave some of his treasure to his wife, Elizabeth, and their three children: seventeen-year-old Abigail, thirteen-year-old Paulsgrave Jr., and eight-year-old John, who lived nearby in Newport. Newport was an active seaport frequented by pirates and privateers from the Caribbean, Madagascar, the Red Sea and the Indian Ocean. His visit would not have turned heads. Although there is no record of his returning to Newport, it is possible that he did and that the record, like so many of the other town records, was destroyed by the British when they marched through during the Revolutionary War. This might explain why the records are silent about him from 1704 when he became a freeman of Newport, to 1715 when he joined up with Bellamy.

Williams would have been the man of his mother's house; the male line of the family had died out more than thirty years ago leaving his mother, the twice-widowed, sixty-seven-year-old Anna (Alcock) Williams Guthrie the matriarch of the family that included her seven children—five daughters and two sons—and twenty-nine grandchildren. Anna may have greeted him wearing her "spectackles," and since it was mid-April and probably chilly because the water temperature in nearby Cape Cod was forty degrees, she might have been wearing the only pair of shoes she owned. She would have been dressed in her simple "waring apparel" that, as one Block Island resident described, was "pale of the blandishments and corruptions of fashion."[10] Her home would have been like all the other Rhode Island homes of the period: a post-and-beam structure covered with shingles with a low stone foundation and center chimney; one-and-a-half stories high with a simple gable roof.[11] Anna's Last Will and Testament told of her practical furnishings that included a feather bed with a feather pillow, two blankets, a bolster, a "new" chest and a close stool.[12] More than likely, the family home would have been the center of a farm, with cleared fields around it and stone walls that marked the property lines. Contained within the property would have been several small outbuildings—barns for her livestock that she listed as "five milch cows, three two year olds, and five one year old cattle," sheds, privy, and corncribs. The earthy smells of hay and animals would have been a drastic change for Williams who spent the last twenty-four months in salty sea spray.

Williams's mother was a very wealthy woman; she inherited land and money not only from her two husbands but also early on from both sides of her highly distinguished English family. Anna and her twin sister, Sarah, were the eldest of the nine children of Dr. John and Sarah (Paulsgrave) Alcock of Roxbury, Massachusetts. The Williams family called Block Island home because Dr. Alcock was one of the original purchasers and settlers of the island. In 1661, he and sixteen others bought Block Island for £400 as a business enterprise to raise sheep and cattle to compete with the butchers in Roxbury, Massachusetts. Dr. Alcock was one of the early graduates of Harvard in 1646 and practiced medicine in Roxbury and later Boston. He was a freeman and a large investor in lands in various parts of New England. In addition to Block Island, he had land in several towns on the eastern coast of Massachusetts, including acreage on Boston Neck, at Dorchester on the Assabet River, in Stow, where he built an estate known as the "Williams Place," and in Scituate near the harbor.[13]

Anna's mother, Sarah, was also a family healthcare provider and her patients described her as "very skillful in physick and chirurgery, exceedingly active, yea unwearied in ministering to ye necessities of others."[14] Anna's grandfather, Dr. Richard Paulsgrave, for whom Williams is named, was the early physician and principle settler of Charleston, Massachusetts.[15] He passed down to his daughter, Sarah Paulsgrave Alcock, a significant amount of land and Anna inherited some of it at the age of fifteen when her mother passed away. Anna's inheritance included a large piece of property on Block Island left to her by her father and to protect her fortune she had a prenuptial agreement drawn up before she married John Williams in 1670 at the age of twenty.[16]

Williams's father, John Williams, had been a successful and prominent Boston merchant with homes in Boston, Newport and Block Island. He was active in public service serving as a freeman from Newport, a representative from Block Island to the Rhode Island General Assembly and in 1686 as the Attorney General. On Block Island he build a wharf and warehouse on four acres of "Fort Island" in Great Salt Pond to store the goods he traded in Barbados.[17] It is very likely that he, like so many Rhode Islanders, evaded the British trade tariffs. He died at the age of forty-four leaving his wife of eighteen years with six children to raise on her own. Paulsgrave was their fourth child, born in 1676, and just eleven years old when his father died. John Williams's Last Will and Testament named Anna and his close friend, Robert Guthrie, co-executors of his large estate and he appointed Guthrie the guardian of his underage children.

In the colonial period, and especially on Block Island, marriage was a necessity rather than a romantic alliance. Large families were common and encouraged because children were needed as laborers on the family farm or as helpers in the family business. Too, women produced many children because so many children did not survive early childhood at that time. John Williams's will, in fact, included an unborn child in the list of his dependents and that child is not listed in the vital records, which means the child did not survive. With so many children, and the demands of everyday life that for women included milking cows, cultivating gardens, spinning yarn, weaving textiles, churning butter, cooking, chopping kindling, and assisting her husband in the running of farms and businesses (legal and illegal), Anna would have needed someone to help her maintain her family. She and Robert Guthrie were married within eighteen months of John Williams's death and Guthrie, a widower, moved the Williams family from Newport, where they had lived for the last several years, and permanently settled them on Block Island.

It was through Robert Guthrie that the Williams family became connected with some of the leading smugglers, money launderers and black marketers in New England.[18] Guthrie was a Scottish exile and one of the groups of Scottish prisoners who were sent over as indentured servants to work at the Braintree Iron Works after the battles of Dunbar and Worcester. Many Scots were taken prisoner by the Parliament and sold for a period of years to a company of London merchants known as Bex & Co. The Scots were shipped to New England to do the hard labor of working the iron deposits in Lynn and Braintree, Massachusetts, near Boston.[19] A native of Edinburgh, he was the son of the Reverend James Guthrie, a minister at Sterling, who, because of his writings, was executed by the English in front of his family when Robert was an infant. (Cromwell described him as the "short man who would not bow.")[20] Guthrie's mother and siblings were banished from the country and they were part of the large contingent of Scottish prisoners of war transported to New England to slave in the Braintree Ironworks.

Guthrie and a number of the Scots eventually relocated to Block Island and were some of the early settlers; they were also part of a community that was gaining a reputation for organized crime.[21]

Guthrie was a freeman and established himself on Block Island working in various capacities including Town Clerk (the early town records are written in his hand), Tax Rater and Overseer of the Poor. Anna and Robert Guthrie had a baby girl named Catherine who was born on Block Island. Catherine was Guthrie's first child—his thirty-one year marriage to his late wife, Margaret Ireland, was without children and at fifty-five years old he was a father with a new bride. Two years later, in 1692, Guthrie was traveling in a small boat returning to Block Island from Newport when a storm whipped up the seas. He was never heard from again.[22]

The loss must have been devastating for Williams, too. Within five years, between the formative years of eleven and sixteen years old, he lost his father and stepfather. It is no surprise, given these circumstances, that he turned pirate. Williams grew up in an environment where the line between legal and respectable work on the one hand, and illegal work on the other, was very ambiguous. Robert Guthrie, for example, performed important public service as Town Clerk and Overseer of the Poor but he also had the reputation of keeping company with shady characters and engaging in illegal activity.[23] John Williams also had straddled both sides of that ambiguous line; he was Attorney General of Rhode Island, but he also evaded the British trade tariffs and kept company with Robert Guthrie, who was part of the New England underworld.

Piracy would not have been a foreign business to Paulsgrave Williams, but as a jeweler by trade, he knew he was not equipped to be a pirate on his own; he needed a partner with maritime experience. "Black Sam" Bellamy was the perfect partner. Piracy was a networked business and pirates knew a lot of people from their previous lives as merchants, jewelers, privateers or seamen. They moved across land and sea easily and for someone like Williams who had been in the business several years, the network of the "brotherhood" was extensive, especially on Block Island.

Anna dictated her Last Will and Testament nine months after Williams's visit and she made clear her deep love and devotion to her very close-knit family. Thoughtfully, she allocated her land, her money, her household furnishings and her personal belongings including her "spectackle box," to her daughters and sons-in-law listing each one by name. She also gave "one good cow" to several of her grandsons, a practical and important gift that ensured their future well-being, because on Block Island a person could survive if he had a cow to milk and use to plow the fields to produce food. She did not gift Williams, perhaps because she thought he did not need her assets, but she did bequeath part of her estate to his two sons, Paulsgrave, Jr. and John. Anna signed her will with her mark, an "X," which meant she was illiterate and could not write her name. But it did not stop her from reflecting on her long life and asking that "… God with his gracious mercy forgive all my sins …"[24] Anna died on Block Island in 1723, five years after Williams's visit at the age of seventy-three.

Years later, in 1741, Williams's wife Elizabeth, still living in Newport, filed a petition with the Newport Town Council requesting that a Newport ship's carpenter named Stephen Hookey be made guardian of the children of Paulsgrave Jr. because he had "gone and left his children"[25] to go Jamaica to make wigs. Hookey was required to put up a £1500 bond for the guardianship of Williams's two grandsons. It is believed that the mother of the boys had died and with their father in Jamaica, a guardian was needed to provide for the young boys.[26] It is very likely that Elizabeth did not have the means or the ability to care for her two young grandsons because she filed the petition by herself, making it clear she was alone and the matriarch of her family at that time.

On the secluded Block Island, close to civilization but far enough away so as not to be under the watchful eyes of the authorities, it was not uncommon to have a family that was a mixed bag of good and bad actors. There were the doctors, civil servants and even the Attorney General on one side and the dark connection to illegal activity, and even a pirate on the other. Block Island went from a place that sponsored the reputable business activity of raising sheep and cattle to tolerating the illegal activities of smuggling and piracy. Dr. John Alcock, wealthy landowner and doctor, and Paulsgrave Williams, pirate, are at opposite ends of the social spectrum. In the middle, between the respectable and not respectable, is Paulsgrave Williams's mother, Anna, a formidable woman, who knew how to survive by straddling both worlds. As a mother and grandmother she provided for her children and grandchildren. As the mother of a pirate she harbored illegal activity and possibly fenced stolen goods. Elizabeth Williams also straddled both worlds: as the wife of a pirate she may have accepted stolen goods from Williams and as a grandmother she took responsible legal action to provide for her grandsons. Clearly, there were strong women who held the Williams family together long after the men had gone.

Before Williams left Block Island, he released Captain Beer and his crew unharmed. Bellamy and Williams had captured Beer's vessel off the coast of South Carolina a week or two prior to Williams's visit to Block Island. After taking the cargo, Williams and Bellamy wanted to give Beer back his ship but the *Whydah* crew objected, fearing Beer would notify the authorities. Williams took Captain Beer and his crew on board the *Marianne,* releasing him upon arrival at his home island. When Beer arrived home eleven days later, on April 29, 1717, one of the first things he did was report to the *Boston News-Letter* his experience with the pirates, grateful that he had been freed unharmed.[27]

Williams sailed out of Block Island's secluded harbor and cruised the mouth of Long Island Sound to Gardiner's Island. From Mary, Williams would have known that Captain Kidd had visited the island in 1699 and left a number of chests and bundles of treasure with the owner of the island, John Gardiner. Williams may likewise have wanted to leave some of his wealth with the proprietor to hold until he collected it at the end of the summer.[28] On April 26, 1717, there was a powerful storm blowing from the southeast. Long Island Sound roiled with whitecaps, and blustery winds threatened Williams' fragile vessel. Williams had already suffered through a previous storm that splintered his mainmast. He found shelter behind Gardiner's Island. Meanwhile Bellamy and the other two pirate ships in the flotilla were along the Atlantic coast of Cape Cod in dense fog and high surf. Soon they were battling a fierce storm that resulted in the *Whydah* shipwreck and a devastating loss of life, including "Black Sam" Bellamy's.

Williams was oblivious to the tragedy. For him, it was business as usual, attacking merchant ships that came within his sight. Two days after the *Whydah* wreck, on April 28, he and the crew of the *Marianne* plundered a sloop from Connecticut, taking three bushels of salt and two of their sailors. One of the sailors, Edward Sargeant, knew the area well and was forced to act as their pilot to help them navigate the waters between Montauk and Martha's Vineyard.[29] On April 29, 1717, Williams was near the entrance to Long Island Sound cruising for prizes. He was still unaware of the Cape Cod catastrophe, even though news of the wreck and the Governor's reaction filled the *Boston News-Letter*.[30] Massachusetts Governor Samuel Shute put the colony on wartime alert; with so many pirates in the area he was concerned for the safety of the sea-lanes.[31] He sent for the fifth-rate frigate HMS *Rose* from the West Indies to protect the New England waters.

The pirates in one of the vessels in Bellamy's flotilla survived the storm and beached near Eastham and Orleans, Cape Cod. Seven of them made a mad dash across the sand and unpaved muddy roads towards Rhode Island, possibly to meet up with Williams and take shelter at his mother's home. A posse from Smith Tavern and Justice Doane, the deputy sheriff, captured the seven pirates at-large on Cape Cod; they were in Barnstable, several miles away from where they had beached. The two survivors of the shipwreck, John Julian and Thomas Davis, were also apprehended and the Governor issued a warrant to Justice Doane on April 29, 1717, ordering him to transport the nine surviving pirates to Barnstable jail, the same jail where Maria Hallett had been detained, until they could be transported under strong security to the Boston jail.

The group reached Boston on May 4, 1717, and for five months they languished in a decrepit jail chained in close quarters and endured sweltering summer heat, poor living conditions and bad food while they awaited their trial. During their stay the Reverend Cotton Mather, a member of Puritan New England's most famous family of clergy and statesmen, visited them frequently, preaching to them sometimes twice a day about their evil ways. Each of the pirates was questioned and their testimony was recorded as a matter of public record. It is from their testimony that we know about the exploits of the pirates, the last moments before the shipwreck and the vast riches that were buried in the sand with the *Whydah*.

On Friday, October 18, 1717, the pirates were brought to trial in the Admiralty Court in Boston. Twelve judges were gathered, including the governor, Samuel Shute. John Julian, the Cape Cod Indian, never went to trial—he mysteriously disappeared from any public record. Some believe he was sold into slavery. Eight pirates went to trial; Thomas Davis was let free on the basis that he had been forced against his will to join the pirates and maintained that claim since he was taken from the *St. Michael.* Thomas South was also acquitted at the trial on the basis that he, like Thomas Davis, was forced to join the pirates. The other six, Simon Van Vorst of New York, John Brown of Jamaica, Thomas Baker of Holland, Hendrick Quintor of Amsterdam, Peter Hoof of Sweden, and John Shuan of Nantes, France were convicted of piracy in the taking of the *Mary Anne.*

On November 15, 1717, the pirates were taken to the North Meeting House where the Reverend Cotton Mather preached a sermon to them while they awaited execution. (The *Whydah* pirates were not the only pirates the Reverend Cotton Mather preached to; he gave sermons to the crew of Captain Kidd, and others, reusing his theme and adapting it to his audience.) The sermon was published in a pamphlet entitled "Instructions to the Living from the Condition of the Dead" and sold for a profit to a wide audience. The prisoners were taken to Charlestown Ferry, an area outside of Boston. The accused, Baker and Hoof, appeared penitent and later joined their fell brethren, Van Vorst, in singing a Dutch psalm.[32] John Brown, however, "broke out into furious expressions with many oaths and then fell to reading prayers," which Cotton Mather described as " 'not very pertinently chosen.' "[33] John Brown then made a short speech in which he advised sailors and listeners to "Beware of wicked living ... Also, if you fall into the hands of pirates, as I did, have a care what countries they came into."[34] In accordance with the law, the pirates were sentenced to hang "within the flux and the reflux of the sea." Their bodies were left hanging from sunset into the early morning. In a terrible twist of fate, just four days before the six pirates were hanged, news reached the city that a British warship had arrived in New York carrying a royal pardon for the condemned men.[35] Their lives could have been spared.

———◆◆◆———

Williams continued to plunder. On May 3, 1717, he found himself south of Martha's Vineyard. He and his crew took two Boston trading sloops inbound from North Carolina, seizing items that would help them careen the *Marianne,* and forced a Devonshire man living in Boston to help them navigate safely around Cape Cod up to Maine.[36] On May 8, 1717, the authorities in Rhode Island fitted out two sloops under the command of Colonel John Cranston and Captain Job Almy to speak with Williams who was lurking on the Rhode Island coast.[37] They did not find him. He was too fast for them and got away. Desperate to find pirates, Governor Shute sent the HMS *Rose* to Cape Cod where she spent nearly three weeks patrolling for pirates, including a day spent hovering near the *Whydah* wreck site.[38]

Two weeks went by and there were no ships to plunder. Around mid-May Williams steered the *Marianne* towards Damariscove Island, Maine, to meet up with Bellamy and the other captains in the flotilla. Damariscove Island was a long rocky island with a snug cove that had been a rendezvous point for mariners for more than a century. Williams waited for Bellamy for five days. On May 21, 1717, Governor Shute learned that Williams had been in the area and he ordered a weeklong closure of Boston Harbor and armed the *Mary Free Love* as a privateer to hunt down Williams. He also sent the HMS *Rose* as support for the *Mary Free Love* and allowed the captain to press twenty of Boston's men to make sure he had enough crew to take on the pirates.[39] All of New England fretted over the potential loss of life and commerce from the sea robbers.

After nearly a week of watching and waiting for his comrades, Williams left Damariscove Island on May 23, 1717, and set a course for Cape Cod. He was forced to conclude something had gone terribly wrong with his comrades. It was now about a month since the *Whydah's* shipwreck, and it is highly likely that Williams learned for the first time the fate of his comrades from Samuel Skinner, the captain of the schooner, *Swallow,* which he seized on May 25th when he was within sight of Cape Cod. Captain Skinner's deposition does not explicitly say he told Williams about the shipwreck—the deposition was brief and very general—still, it is highly likely he told Williams, not because he would have known the two men knew each other, but because it was the talk of the town in every seaport along the New England coast. Skinner later testified that Williams released him without harm and sailed out of the bay.[40] Williams returned to the *Whydah* wreck site on several occasions. His visits were either for sentimental reasons or to try to retrieve his share of the stolen loot. Like Cyprian Southack, who was sent by the Governor to retrieve pirate loot for the crown, he was unable to get near the sunken vessel due to the strong winds and waves that churned the frigid water into a threatening death pool. The grisly end to a successful partnership with his friend "Black Sam" Bellamy must have been sobering and heart-wrenching, but it did not stop Williams. He set out on the *Marianne* and continued plundering merchant vessels for another two years.

In June 1717, Williams was off New York and he was desperately in need of water for his crew. While Williams was bartering for it with another ship captain, two of his crewmembers, Richard Caverley, Williams's master, and Jeremiah Higgins, his boatswain, jumped ship and an elaborate manhunt took place throughout New England for the runaway pirates. (This is the same Jeremiah Higgins who disclosed that Williams visited his mother and sisters on Block Island.) Meanwhile, Williams continued plundering down the Eastern seaboard into the Bahamas.

While all of this was going on, Captain Woods Rogers arrived in New Providence, Bahamas, with orders from the Crown to end piracy by administering the King's Pardon.[41] The King's proclamation of September 5, 1717, allowed pirates a year to turn them themselves in and receive a pardon. In February 1718, Williams was in Nassau and he "came in," which meant he surrendered himself to the governor of Bermuda and took the King's pardon. By taking the pardon, Williams understood that all would be forgiven and there would be no consequences for his past piratical activities if he promised never to return to piracy. Williams could not keep his promise for long, and in 1719 he was reported off the coast of Africa serving as a quartermaster of a pirate ship captained by his old friend from the Hornigold days, Oliver Levasseur, known as "La Buze." William Snelgrave, a slave captain whose ship the *Bird* was captured by "La Buze" in the Sierra Leone River on April Fool's Day, 1719, and released a month later, wrote of his experience with the pirates and reported that Williams was "grouchy and despondent and threatened him with violence without provocation." He said another captive told him, "Do not be afraid of him, for it is his usual way of talking.... be sure to call him Captain."[42] Williams apparently warmed to those who called him his old rank because he was unhappy being second in command rather than captain. Snelgrave called him Captain Williams and Williams gave him a keg of wine and Snelgrave wrote that Williams "was my Friend ever after."

Some pirates die on the gallows or in shipwrecks, but Williams did neither of these. He simply disappeared. He was last seen in April 1719. Some believe he drowned.[43] If this is the case, he would have been about forty-three years old when he went to a watery grave to join his friend "Black Sam" Bellamy.

It was a lucky move for Williams when he veered away from his partner Samuel Bellamy and his comrades and went to Block Island to visit his mother and sisters. It was pure chance that he would become such an important eighteenth-century pirate, providing a window into his family, especially his mother and sisters, and his home on Block Island. The story of Captain Paulsgrave Williams sheds light on the extensive web of support pirates had and relied on from women.

Despite the dangerous and disordered patterns Williams participated in by following plunder where ever it may be, and the unpredictable occurrences that happened, such as bad weather and a shipwreck that jolted the career of a pirate and his band, Williams still maintained relationships with his mother and kin, confirming the importance of women in this pirate's life. Williams's sisters were not just helpmates to him; they were involved with other pirates—Captain Kidd and members of his crew. And it is very likely they knew some of the *Whydah* pirates because the Williams's home on Block Island was a well-known safe refuge and an easy place to unload stolen cargo. The *Whydah* pirates on the run from the authorities tried hard to reach the Williams's home but were apprehended on Cape Cod before they could reach Rhode Island. An important trait in the Williams family was trust and loyalty and it bound the web of networks together. The Williams women were silent partners and they left little evidence behind. But they were not only family members; they were agents participating in the business of piracy. Now we know how profoundly important women were to many pirates; pirates not only needed them, they relied on them. And we may never have known this if Paulsgrave Williams had followed "Black Sam" Bellamy to Cape Cod.

CHAPTER 3

The Woman Behind the Pirate

Captain William Kidd

Nowhere in the Last Will and Testament of Sarah Rousby is there the slightest hint of her previous life. At the age of seventy-four, Sarah summarized her long life in a few short sentences:

> "In the name of God, Amen. I, Sarah Rousby of New York, widow of Christopher Rousby, late of New Jersey, deceased, being in good health and perfect mind. The funerals of my body are to be only such as shall become a Christian. After the payment of all debts and funeral charges, I leave all the rest of ye estate to my five children, Christopher Rousby, Henry Rousby, Sarah, widow of Joseph Latham, late of New York, William Rousby, and Elizabeth, wife of John Troup, Jr. My eldest son Christopher shall have my wedding ring. I make my eldest son Christopher and my son-in-law John Troup, executors. My houses and lands are to be sold by my executors."[1]

What is telling here is not what Sarah wrote, but what she didn't. You see, history records that Sarah's life was not as simple as her will implies, nor was her life as ordinary as she made it out to be. Christopher Rousby was Sarah's fourth husband. Before she was Sarah Rousby, she was Sarah Kidd, wife of Captain William Kidd, one of the most notorious pirates in history.

Famous as an iconic figure who buried treasure and had grand and terrifying adventures on the high seas, Captain Kidd (1645–1701), was infamous in the eyes of the law and the colonial authorities. The story most people know is of Captain Kidd the privateer and pirate hunter who ultimately crossed the line and turned pirate. As a result of this story of treachery, he is often considered America's most ruthless pirate. But as we know, there are often two sides to a pirate story, and Captain Kidd is no exception. What many people don't know is that there was a woman behind this man who pleaded, cajoled, and bribed colonial officials to try to save her husband's life. If Sarah Kidd's initials, "SK," had not been scratched on a few colonial documents, Sarah may have remained invisible in history. But Captain Kidd's involvement in one of the most publicized political scandals that involved top officials on both sides of the Atlantic from London to Boston meant that Sarah went from a young twenty-something New York socialite married to a successful and respected privateer to a pirate's wife and an accomplice to a man on the run from the law. For six years, Captain Kidd was embroiled in a drama that was laced with lies, secrets, double-dealing and betrayal. Sarah may have been illiterate and could only write her initials, like so many women in her time, but her initials mark the spot where love and law divide.

It began on Saturday, May 16, 1691. Captain William Kidd, a tall, well-built, well-dressed forty-six-year-old sea captain with a hint of a Scottish accent married the English born Sarah Bradley Cox Oort, a twice-widowed, wealthy twenty-one-year-old considered one of the most eligible and sought-after women in New York. The day was one of high drama and grisly seventeenth-century justice. The self-appointed Governor Jacob Leisler and his son-in-law, Jacob Milbourne, were hanged for treason against King William and Queen Mary. Sarah and Kidd attended the hanging after their wedding. The stark contrast of the day—a love match and an execution—foreshadowed the dark drama that would be their life together.

In 1695, with England at war with France and pirates plundering British shipping in the East Indies infuriating the East

India Company, Captain Kidd was issued a privateering commission, a legal document officially called a "letter of marque and reprisal" authorizing him to capture enemy French ships. Privateers were like an auxiliary navy that was used when the resources of warring countries were stretched to the limit. A group of investors would supply a ship and hire a captain and crew to seek out and capture England's enemies. The prizes were delivered to the British Admiralty Court where the value of the prizes was assessed and a percentage was given to the investors. Kidd was essentially given permission to act as a pirate by capturing ships and cargo but since he had legal authorization in a letter of marque he was not a pirate, he was considered a privateer. As long as he stuck to the assignment of only capturing French ships, he was legal in the eyes of the law. If he strayed and pursued non-enemy ships he would be considered a pirate out to take the prize for himself and his crew rather than for king and country. Kidd had years of experience as a privateer and his backers were confident he would successfully find prizes and make them rich. They were so sure of Kidd's ability as a master mariner they gave him a second assignment and that was to help clear the seas of pirates. He was to be a pirate hunter. Several pirates in the Red Sea were particularly troublesome to British trade and his letter of marque specifically mentioned that he go after the notorious rogues Thomas Tew, John Ireland, Thomas Wake and William Maze.

Kidd's privateering commission to capture French ships was not a typical letter of marque, however. Imagining the potential for great profits if Kidd succeeded at his mission, some of the most powerful men in England formed a syndicate to sponsor Kidd's voyage. His backers included several prominent members of the ruling Whig party including the Irish nobleman, Richard Coote, Earl of Bellomont, who was soon to be the Governor of Massachusetts, New Hampshire and New York. Also in the syndicate was Edmund Harrison, a wealthy London merchant and a director of the East India Company, King William III, and Colonel Robert Livingston, whose idea it was for Kidd to take the job because Kidd knew the pirates and where they rendezvoused and he would be certain to capture many of them. What made this arrangement so unusual was not only the high profile members, but the special dispensation they gave themselves from the normal privateering terms that required that all prizes be declared at the British Admiralty Court. The syndicate bypassed the Admiralty Court so they could keep all the profits for themselves. Already Kidd's assignment was loaded with potential problems if it became public that some of the most important men in England, including the king, were involved in a money making proposition that profited from the war.

Kidd had just spent five years at home in New York with Sarah and their children working as a merchant captain trading in Antigua. He was anxious to get back into the action of privateering and this opportunity appeared to be the one he had been waiting for. Kidd accepted the privateering commission in April 1696, and armed with the documents spelling out his orders he set sail from the London shipyard in the brand new *Adventure Galley*, a 287 ton vessel that could be rowed as well as sailed, and equipped with thirty-four big guns. He sailed back to New York to recruit his crew for the voyage and to see his family.

Kidd spent several months at home in Manhattan with Sarah and their two daughters, Sarah and Elizabeth, while he readied for his privateering voyage. They lived in a splendid waterfront mansion located at the corner of Pearl and Hanover Streets and the three-story dormered brick home faced the city wall—later to be renamed Wall Street.

An inventory of the house listed luxurious furnishings that kept the Kidd's staff busy polishing the silver, ironing linens for the four feather beds, dusting the dozens of chairs, shaking out the rare Turkish rug, winding the clock, cleaning the looking-glasses, setting out the pewter plates, dishes and glassware to serve more than a dozen guests, and making sure the coat of arms of Kidd's Scottish ancestry was prominently displayed.[2]

Home of Captain and Mrs. William Kidd in 1699. Courtesy of the Library of Congress.

The Pearl Street mansion was one of the several properties Sarah inherited from her first husband, William Cox, an elderly wealthy flour merchant Sarah married when she was fifteen years old. (It is widely believed this was an arranged marriage.) Cox and Sarah were married for four years when he died unexpectedly while on a public errand informing the residents of East Jersey that William and Mary had ascended the throne. Cox's Last Will and Testament left Sarah half of his large fortune, which consisted primarily of six parcels of prime New York real estate and about £1900, a considerable amount of money for that time.[3] Obtaining her inheritance from Cox would be the bane of her existence for many years because at the time of Cox's death in 1689, the government of New York province under the

leadership of Jacob Leisler and his cronies instituted bureau-
cratic red tape that tied up Cox's estate. Sarah could live in Cox's
home on Pearl Street (which is now No. 56 Wall Street) but she
could not have his money and other properties despite the efforts of Captain Kidd and his trusted lawyer and friend, James
Emott, to settle the estate.

A year or so after Cox's death, Sarah married a Dutch merchant
named John Oort. She and Oort were married only a year when
Oort died of unknown causes. Unbeknownst to Sarah, he had bor-
rowed money to pay their bills and she was left alone again at
twenty years old, and heavily in debt. When Sarah met Captain
Kidd is uncertain. Kidd had recently returned to New York after a
successful privateering voyage defending the island of Nevis in the
Caribbean against the French. Certainly she would have met him
while she was still married to Oort. A war hero with a confident
air about him would have caught any woman's eye. Sarah's wedding license says she married Kidd two days after Oort's death.
Some people were dubious about the timing of Sarah's marriage
to Kidd so soon after the death of her second husband but foul
play was never proved and no one really suspected anything was
amiss because Kidd was a highly respected member of New York
polite society. Kidd was so highly regarded the municipal clerk
listed Kidd's occupation as "gent" for gentleman instead of
"mariner" on the marriage license.[4] In keeping with his status, the
gentleman in Kidd paid off all of Oort's debts with his earnings as
a privateer to make Sarah whole.

As the time grew closer for Captain Kidd's departure, he
moved aboard the *Adventure Galley* to make the final prepara-
tions for the voyage. Sarah joined him temporarily while he was
moored in the harbor. Kidd fitted out his ship with supplies and
gear and organized his crew. The terms of the letter of marque
stipulated that the captain and crew would be paid under the
"no purchase no pay" provision. One hundred and fifty-five
men eagerly signed the ship's articles committing themselves to
the rules of Kidd's ship. They were certain they would capture
prizes since they were sailing with Captain Kidd, the noted and

respected privateer. The men were so confident they were going to get rich many turned down a secure salaried position in the colonial militia for this risky adventure on the high seas. In September 1696, Sarah said good-bye to Kidd and her younger brother, twenty-one-year-old Samuel Bradley, Jr., who had joined the crew. As they sailed out of the harbor Sarah knew it would be at least a year, probably more, before she saw him again. Little Sarah and Elizabeth may have been too young to notice his departure.

Captain Kidd and his crew stopped several times for food and supplies before finally dropping anchor on the west coast of Madagascar to let his men, many sick with scurvy, recover from the four-month voyage. Many didn't, however, and fifty men died from the disease within a week of their landing.[5] Kidd was forced to take on more crew, a number of whom were former pirates. After months at sea with no plunder, the men were restless.

Kidd headed to the Red Sea where pirates, especially those mentioned in his letter of marque—Thomas Tew, William Maze and Thomas Wake—preyed on ships carrying goods from East India. The booty supplied the active black market in New York.[6] In early August 1697, Kidd came across the pilgrim fleet leaving Mocha under the protection of three European ships. It was not covered in either of Kidd's privateering commissions—they were not French and they were not pirates—they were merely ships ferrying the faithful and their offerings. But things were tense with Kidd's crew. It had been nearly a year with no plunder and the men worried they would go home penniless. One of the European escorts flying the flag of the East India Company saw Kidd close to the convoy. The captain fired several cannon shots at Kidd warning him to stay away and ordered his men to yell threats of more firepower if he did not retreat. Kidd sailed away.

The *Adventure Galley* was now leaking, and the crew was mutinous and desperately low in supplies. Kidd came across a small trading vessel flying English flags off the Malabar Coast. Finding that her pass was good, Kidd intended to let her go, he said, but then got word that they had Greeks and Armenians on board who were carrying precious stones and other rich goods.[7] What happened next was a turning point for Kidd. His men tortured the crew to find out where the valuables were hidden. Kidd claimed he tried to stop the men, arguing that he did not have a commission to take Englishmen or lawful traders but only permission to plunder the King's enemies and pirates. The crew did not care. Kidd said he could barely restrain the men "from their unlawful designe" but he finally did and let the English ship go.[8] It was not long before the news of Kidd's attempt at the pilgrim fleet and the attack on the English trading vessel spread to the nearby region. Kidd had crossed the fine line between privateer and pirate. The Viceroy of Goa sent two Portuguese naval vessels to battle with Kidd. The naval ships fired six cannon at the *Adventure Galley*, wounding eleven of Kidd's men in a daylong fight.[9] Kidd managed to escape after firing several penetrating cannon shots at the smaller war ship.

A year passed and Kidd still did not have much to show for his efforts. Kidd's men continued to get worse and after landing at the Laccadive Islands the crew went out of control. They seized the local boats and chopped them up for firewood, raped the native women and when the local men retaliated by killing the cooper on Kidd's ship, his crew attacked the village and its inhabitants.[10] Inevitably, news of this atrocity by Kidd's undisciplined and piratical crew reached the mainland, and his reputation was solidified.

In late October 1697, near the coast of Malabar, Kidd got into an argument with his insubordinate gunner, William Moore. Moore had a reputation for being indignant and irascible. The crew had been complaining about the lack of prizes and Moore and Kidd exchanged heated words. In a fit of anger, reported an eyewitness, Kidd hit Moore over the head with an iron-hooped wooden bucket. Moore died the next day. Kidd later testified that Moore was mutinous and had to be disciplined, but he did not, in any way, intend to kill him—that it was a shipboard accident.[11] But as word traveled from port to port, the story different with every teller until it reached London, the authorities labeled Kidd a premeditated murderer. It is uncertain if Sarah heard the rumors that her husband had been accused of murder.

In February 1698, Kidd came across another ship worth capturing as a prize. The *Quedah Merchant* was off the Malabar Coast of India and was loaded with silk, calico, sugar, opium and iron. She had an English captain, Armenian owners and part of the ship's cargo belonged to a senior official at the court of the Mogul of India. Kidd carried flags from various countries as a decoy and flew French flags as he approached the ship. Seeing the French flags, even though the ship was not French, the captain issued him a "French pass" (the ship's registration) to avoid being captured. This played right into Kidd's hands. This would be the second of the two French passes Kidd would collect and hold to prove he had acted within the terms of his letter of marque. Kidd swayed between behaving legally and illegally—he was in a gray area. At times he was a privateer and others times he was a pirate. He was acting within the terms of his letter of marque when he captured French ships and he had proof with the French passes they gave him. But he also pursued non-French ships that pitted him against the legal terms of his commission. Kidd escorted the *Quedah Merchant* and crew to the nearest port, sold the bulk of the cargo to raise much needed cash and with £7000, set out to look for more prizes.

Kidd returned to Sainte-Marie Island in Madagascar in April 1698 and stayed there for several months to regroup and wait for favorable winds. Sainte-Marie was a long, narrow island off the northeast coast of Madagascar where pirates had a well-established settlement and a deep harbor convenient for loading and unloading cargo. There was steady traffic from New York trading vessels bringing supplies to the pirates to sustain their merry lifestyle. Far be it for the pirates not to have some good rum, Madeira wine and barrels and barrels of beer. Kidd complied with the demands of his mutinous men and gave them their share of the plunder, then ninety-seven of his crewmen abandoned him. Gabriel Loffe and Martin Skines received their shares and arranged to put some of their cloth bales into sea chests and sent them home on one of the trading ships from New York.[12] Kidd said his former crew violently threatened his life and took away his journal of his voyage.[13] Reduced to a crew of less than twenty, and faced with a ship badly in need of repair, Kidd swapped the *Adventure Galley* for his prize the *Quedah Merchant,* renamed her the *Adventure Prize* and after five months, he finally got a fair wind and sailed for the West Indies.

Serious news awaited Kidd when he arrived at the island of Anguilla in early April 1699. Responding to complaints by the East India Company (of which one of Kidd's sponsors was a director), the British government had declared him a pirate and the Lord Justices sent word to all the sheriffs in the North American colonies to apprehend him. Desperately in need of refuge, he sailed to the Danish island of St. Thomas where to his chagrin, he was denied protection. Kidd stayed only four hours and quickly headed to the southeastern part of Hispaniola where he moored the *Adventure Prize* in a river and met up with a trader named Henry Bolton, someone who didn't mind dealing with a man who had been declared a pirate. Kidd's ship was leaky and he needed another one to ensure he could escape the authorities who were everywhere in the Caribbean looking for him. Bolton agreed to buy the *Adventure Prize* and the cargo left over from when it was the *Quedah Merchant.* With the proceeds, Kidd bought another vessel, the *Saint Antonio,* and with few other places to turn, sailed up the New England coast to talk to his last hope — Lord Bellomont, his business partner and now Governor of Massachusetts, to convince him that he was not a pirate and to plead for his support.

When Kidd originally wrote to Lord Bellomont asking for his help, he received a carefully worded letter back implying that if he would return to Boston Bellomont would protect him from the authorities.[14] Kidd arrived in the area of Long Island in June 1699 and sent word to his family and friends he was in home waters. He waited for his old trusted friends James Emott, an aggressive elderly gentleman unafraid to battle the authorities, and Duncan Campbell, a fellow Scot and Boston's postmaster with an ear for the latest news, to come aboard the *Saint Antonio* for a strategy session about what he should do to protect himself from the charge of piracy. As loyal confidantes, they would be his go-betweens with the new governor.

At Kidd's request, Emott made arrangements for the now twenty-eight-year-old Sarah to travel secretly from New York to Block Island with their two daughters and her maid, Elizabeth Morris, an English spinster who was an indentured servant to Captain Kidd. Sarah left behind her housekeeper, Dorothy Lee, to mind the Pearl Street residence. Knowing that his wife would be staying with their friends, Edward and Mary (Williams) Sands, (Paulsgrave Williams's older sister), Captain Kidd had already left at their home two cannon weighing 300-pounds each and plenty of ammunition.[15] Kidd was planning for every possibility and the cannon were extra protection for his family as well as a backup supply of firepower in case he had to change ships and make a fast getaway from the authorities. Sarah invited her hosts Edward and Mary to join her at the reunion with her husband on his sloop. Captain Kidd sent men to fetch the group and row them out to the *Saint Antonio* anchored off the east end of Block Island. Already on board were James Emott, Duncan Campbell and sixteen of Kidd's crew.

It had been three years since Sarah had seen her husband. The last time Sarah had seen Kidd he was a privateer hired by the king to capture enemy ships and hunt down pirates; now he was an accused pirate. When Kidd had left Sarah on the dock at New York harbor she was a socialite married to one of the leading citizens in the colony, now she was a pirate's wife. Their roles had changed so dramatically and without warning; now their circumstances were terribly complicated and dangerous. All conversations were shrouded in secrecy and marked with fear over what could be the worst-case scenario—that Captain Kidd would be tried and convicted of piracy.

Sarah followed the instructions she was given to the tee. She was to pack for more than a short visit which meant that if the situation turned sour, she needed to be prepared to seize any available option to stay safely away from the authorities. Sarah packed all the family silver, 260 pieces of eight, a tankard, some eating utensils, and clothes for the children and herself. Kidd, in preparation of seeing Sarah, took out his waistcoat from his trunk and asked James Emott to bring him a wig so he would look his best for her. The only picture of Kidd shows him in a shoulder length light brown wig parted down the middle. He had a large nose and dark eyes. There are no pictures of Sarah but Frederick de Peyster described her in his book on Lord Bellomont as "a lovely and accomplished woman."[16] She also must have been very attractive since she wooed three husbands. New York women of Sarah's social status wore brightly colored dresses cinched at the waist with a bustle and many petticoats that puffed up the floor-length skirt. Sarah would have worn a high fashion dress especially one with an eye-catching low lace neckline.

Kidd's trusted advisors set to work. Campbell delivered Kidd's letters of protestation and negotiation to Lord Bellomont. He reminded him of Kidd's good character and reputation, noting that Kidd had received a ship from the Governor of Nevis in 1689 for his bravery and leadership fighting as a British privateer against the French. For his services in quelling the disturbances in the colony of New York after the revolution of 1688, the Council of New York awarded him £150. He was a respected merchant trader who made regular trips to the Caribbean to drop cargo in Antigua, and when he was in port, he helped build Trinity Church, served as a foreman on a Grand Jury, and spent time with his wife, his young daughters and his brother-in-law who he mentored like a son. It was no accident he was chosen to captain the *Adventure Galley*, he had a proven track record of dependability and honesty. His character was so impeccable the King of England issued him a letter of marque.

Emott also met with Lord Bellomont and gave him the two French passes that showed, without a doubt, that Kidd had acted as a privateer. Lord Bellomont was well aware of the terms of Kidd's letter of marque, he had signed on four years ago as one of his sponsors hoping Kidd would make him rich. Seriously in need of money, he had put his bet on Kidd to make him financially whole. But things had changed, he was now the Governor of Massachusetts and beholden to His Majesty's government. He had orders to apprehend Kidd and whatever his feelings for Kidd, he would obey his king and send him to stand trial for piracy in England.

Just in case, Kidd safeguarded his treasure by stashing it away in various places with trusted friends. Kidd told Sarah where most of it was. He sailed the *Saint Antonio* to Gardiner's Island, an island three miles north of Long Island near the entrance to Long Island Sound.[17] The 3300-acre wooded estate was known for its secluded location and the warm hospitality of its owner, John Gardiner. It is there Kidd buried a chest with forty pounds of gold and 300–400 pieces of eight.[18] The chest was nailed shut, tied with a cord, and fastened with a padlock so no one but Kidd could open it. He gave Gardiner a small chest that contained some of his most valuable possessions; three small bags of Jasper Antonio or stone of Goa (a fever medicine consisting of various drugs made up into a hard ball made by the Jesuits of Goa), several pieces of silk with silver and gold stripes, spices including a bushel of cloves and nutmegs mixed together, fine white calicoes and muslins and flowered silk.[19] He also left a bundle of nine or ten fine India quilts, some of them made of silk with fringes and tassels.[20] Anticipating that it would be difficult to obtain food, Captain Kidd asked Mrs. Gardiner to prepare a pig for him, as well as for six sheep for his trip to Boston and a barrel of cider. He also asked Gardiner for a boat to take him to Boston.[21] John Gardiner later testified that as a thank you for preparing a pig, Captain Kidd gave Mrs. Gardiner a pitcher and several pieces of damaged gold muslin cloth, which despite their condition were considered valuable items.[22] Captain Kidd offered to pay Gardiner for the cider but Gardiner said the gift to his wife was enough.

It was sometime during his stopover at Gardiner's Island that Captain Kidd penned a response to Lord Bellomont's letter. Duncan Campbell departed for Boston to deliver it to Bellomont along with a gift of an enameled box with four jewels in it for his wife, the Countess Bellomont. As Captain Kidd lingered between Gardiner's Island and Block Island, three sloops came alongside his sloop and removed some of his passengers and crew plus their sea chests and a share of the cargo.[23] Sarah also made some precautionary withdrawals sending along with Thomas Way, a master mariner from Boston, the six-pound bag of pieces of eight she brought with her from New York. Thomas Way later testified that he saw Captain Kidd again off Nantucket as the captain was sailing towards Boston and that Kidd gave him three pistols, a balance scale to weigh gold, a turkey carpet, a clock, a small bundle of clothes and some coins.[24] Kidd asked him to deliver the parcels to Sarah to ensure she was comfortable and could pay her expenses should anything happen to him.

Captain Kidd arrived in Boston the next day, June 28, 1699, and he and his family stayed at Duncan Campbell's house in Boston. It was the first time since 1696 that they had been a family together onshore. They walked the narrow streets of Boston, attended church together and Captain Kidd, at liberty in town, frequented the Blue Anchor Tavern.[25] As a thank you to his hostess Captain Kidd gave Duncan Campbell's wife, Mrs. Susannah Campbell, a gold chain, a piece of India silk and three pieces of muslin.[26]

Kidd was asked to appear before the Governor's Council on July 3rd to give an account of his three-year voyage. He testified that his journal had been violently destroyed by his crew at Sainte-Marie but if he was granted the time he would prepare a written narrative giving a complete account of his activities.[27] Captain Kidd completed the narrative of his activities and was called to testify before the Council two more times.[28] Lord Bellomont, who suffered from gout, a painful condition that affected his feet and hands, observed that Kidd "seemed much disturbed ... and fancied he looked as if he were upon the wing."[29] Fearing that Kidd was going to run away, Lord Bellomont and the members of the Council decided it would be best if Kidd were seized and committed to Boston Jail.

On July 6, 1699 Captain Kidd was arrested in Boston at the Governor's house while trying to interview Lord Bellomont about his aloof behavior towards him. Captain Kidd was put in solitary confinement in the stone prison in Boston and chained to a sixteen-pound weight. Lord Bellomont stated in a letter that month to the Board of Trade in London that one reason he did not arrest Kidd earlier is "... he had brought his wife and children hither in the sloop with him, who I believed he would not easily forsake."[30] It is a telling statement from a man who proclaimed in the same month to the Lords of Trade in London, "There never was a greater liar or thief in the world than this Kidd."[31] One has to wonder if Bellomont had trouble justifying the villainous image of a pirate with a man who has his wife and two daughters onboard ship with him.

Magistrates and officers immediately went to Duncan Campbell's house and seized all of Captain Kidd's assets and they took personal belongings and household articles belonging to Sarah and Elizabeth Morris. The seizure made it abundantly clear that Sarah's legal status had changed and she was now considered an accessory to a criminal. Whatever the authorities said about pirates as social isolates without connections on land was now totally false—the Kidds were considered a criminal couple.

Duncan Campbell urged Sarah to send a letter to the Governor's Council to petition Lord Bellomont to return her belongings. It was risky for Campbell to involve himself in the affairs of a couple in trouble with the law, but rather than shy away from the Kidds, he gave Sarah detailed advice on how to go about approaching the Governor and his Council. Her petition is in the Massachusetts Archives and reads:[32]

> To his Excellency the Earl of Bellomont, Captn. Gen. and Govr. In Chief of his Maj'tys provinces of the Massachusetts Bay, New Yorke, etca. In America, and of the Territorys thereon depending, and Vice Admiral of the same,

> The petition of Sarah Kidd, the wife of Captain Wm. Kidd: Humbly Sheweth:

> That on the sixth day of July Inst., some of the Magisrates and officers of this place came into your Pet'rs lodgings at the house of Duncan Campbell, and did there seize and take out of a Trunck, a Silver Tankard, a Silver Mugg, a Silver Porringer and Spoons, forcks, and 260 Pieces of Eight, yr. Pet'rs sole and proper Plate and mony, brought With her from New York, whereof she has had the possion of for several years past, as she can truly make oath; out of which sd
> Trunck was also took Twenty five English Crowns which Belonged to your Pet'rs Maid.

*The premises and most deplorable Condition of yr. Pet'r
Considered, She humbly intreats your hon'rs Justice, That
Returne be made of the said Plate and mony.*

Sarah X SK X Kidd

With Kidd in prison, Sarah needed money to live on. She knew
her husband had stashed nearly three pounds of gold with Captain
Thomas Paine, a retired Rhode Island pirate. She would get word
to him through the pirate network.

Paine had gone to Rhode Island in 1683 as a privateer with ques-
tionable papers. He chose Rhode Island as his home because it was
the colony that had welcomed pirates for decades. Very quickly Captain Paine shed his pirate life and remade himself into a model citizen. He married Mercy Carr, the daughter of the Governor of Rhode
Island, Caleb Carr, served on the Grand Jury, was appointed tax as-
sessor, was admitted as a freeman, and was one of the founders of
Trinity Church in Newport. (Paine and six other pirates founded the
church and their names are on a plaque outside the church today.)
Because of his naval warfare experience he was asked in 1689 to lead
an expedition to fight the French privateers who attacked nearby
Block Island.[33] He and his crew, which included his father-in-law and
two brothers-in-law, successfully defeated the French and his valor
and leadership raised his reputation to that of an eminent citizen.

In June 1699, this eminently respected member of the community received an unexpected visitor—Captain Kidd. The Paines
lived comfortably on a farm on the north end of Conanicut Island,
near Jamestown, Rhode Island. Their unique two storey home with
an overhanging roof overlooked Narragansett Bay and the shoreline was just a few hundred feet from their front door. The knock
on the door was from a Kidd crewmember asking Paine if he would
meet with Kidd on his sloop—the matter was urgent.

Kidd asked the grizzled sixty-seven-year-old ex-pirate if he would
safeguard some gold and dispense it to the proper messenger when
the time was right. James Gilliam, who had been on board Captain
Kidd's ship at the time of the reunion with Sarah, was with Captain
Kidd and asked Paine to hold 800 pieces of eight.[34] Captain Paine
became (or possibly always was?) known as the pirates' banker. It is

not known how Captain Kidd and Paine met, but it is evident that Captain Kidd's social network was large and long-standing. Captain Kidd knew just where to find the old pirate and did not hesitate to ask his friend for help. Receiving and concealing stolen goods was a capital offense that would have dismissed all of Paine's good deeds, but Paine did not hesitate, as there was loyalty among mariners.

Lord Bellomont, following Kidd's trail from a tip by Colonel Sanford, Judge of the Admiralty Court in Rhode Island,[35] tried three or four times to depose Captain Paine but Paine refused. It was only under threat of going to jail that Paine swore that he rebuffed Captain Kidd's request to conceal his gold because the authorities would search his house. That, of course, was a lie; he did not refuse Kidd but he was in a tough spot and the choice was either to lie or get arrested for concealing stolen goods. At the time, a lie seemed the lesser of two evils.

While she was briefly held in Boston prison, Sarah sent a letter to Thomas Paine dated July 18, 1699. As per Kidd's arrangement with Paine, Sarah asked him to give seven bars of gold weighing 24 ounces to Andrew Knott, a pirate who lived in Boston and who was a friend and associate of James Gilliam. Sarah asked Paine to keep the rest of the gold in his custody until further notice "for it is all we have to support us in time of want."[36] Paine understood the seriousness of her request; Captain Kidd had made it very clear during his visit to Paine's farm that stashing gold with Paine was a backup plan to protect his wife and family in case of emergency. With both of them in jail it was an emergency and they had to tap into their reserves. Sarah's letter to Captain Paine reads:[37]

From Boston Prison, July ye 18 day 1699.

Capt Payen,
After my humble service to your selfe and all our good
Friends this cometh by a trusty Friend of mine how [sic] can
declare to you of my great griefe and misery here in prison
by how I would desire you to send me Twenty four ounces of
Gold and as for all ye rest you have in your custody shall de-
sire you for to keep in your custody for it is all we have to
support us in time of want; but I pray you to deliver to the

*bearer hereof the above mentioned sum, hows [sic]name is
Andrew Knott. And in so doing you will oblige him how is
you're the bare hereof can informe you more at large.*

Sarah X SK X Keede.

In one of the many lengthy letters Lord Bellomont wrote to the
Board of Trade, he said that while he was searching for the noto-
rious James Gilliam in Boston, he searched Captain Andrew
Knott's house and inadvertently found in a small trunk Sarah
Kidd's letter to Captain Paine among some remnants of East India
goods.[38] Knott was hiding his connection with the Kidds; he also
was hiding his association with Captain Gilliam and lied to Lord
Bellomont that he had any knowledge of him. It was not until
Lord Bellomont interviewed Mrs. Knott that the truth came out
and she confessed that the married pirate James Gilliam had stayed
with them several nights and that he was not far from their house
but was busy being "friendly" with two young women.

Knott reported to Bellomont that he went to Captain Paine's
house at Sarah's request and was given 7 bars of gold weighing 1¾
lbs. Paine fetched the gold from a bedroom in the back of the
house. On the road home, Knott claimed, the weight of the gold
broke through his pocket and he lost one of the gold bars. The
other six he brought to Boston and Captain Kidd's maid, Rebecca,
collected the gold from him and gave him 24 pieces of eight for
undertaking the five-day journey.[39]

Sarah noticed the amount of gold was short by a few ounces and
she told Captain Knott the six bars of gold weighed 21½ or 22
ounces not the 24 ounces she requested. Knott did not say what
happened to the lost seventh bar of gold but one might suspect that
it was transferred to the pirate's other pocket. Sarah's letter to Captain Paine and her astute accounting of the missing gold sheds light
on her strong business acumen and her determination to protect
herself and her family during this difficult period. The partnership
between Captain Kidd and Sarah cannot be overlooked. The couple
worked in tandem with Kidd providing the gold and the plan with
Paine and Sarah activating the plan with Knott as the intermediary.

As the Kidds waited in a state of limbo for the outcome of their future, there was one good piece of news: Sarah's petition to Lord Bellomont requesting that her things be returned was honored. The letter dated July 25, 1699, from the Council said "The household plate from New Yorke by Captain Kidd's wife, seized with Money and treasure, be restored unto her, and that the hat and wearing apparel (under seizure) belonging to Captain Kidd and his company, be delivered unto him."[40] A chest was also restored to Captain Kidd that had been taken from the *Saint Antonio* and contained his own property.

In addition to getting her belongings back, Sarah was released from prison. She very quickly sent another petition to Lord Bellomont and the Council asking if she could visit her husband in jail. He had been in solitary confinement for two weeks, sweating in the July heat and was in need of fresh clothes and "affection."[41] Suspecting that Sarah and Kidd would collude on an escape plan, Bellomont did not allow her to visit and in fact had Kidd moved deeper into the prison so that Sarah could not yell to him through the window. Sarah and the children moved out of Duncan Campbell's home into a humble waterfront inn,[42] a far cry from her waterfront mansion on Pearl Street. Months passed and Sarah waited for her husband to be released. In late fall, Sarah put in a petition to the Council requesting that they supply warm clothes to Kidd so he would not continue to suffer on the cold damp stone floor. There is no record the request was ever approved. Kidd spent all but thirty minutes a day in solitary confinement and he still professed he was not a pirate and that he had not committed a crime that would warrant his arrest.

Christmas 1699 was a non-event for the Kidds. He had been in prison five months and Sarah and the girls were in a holding pattern waiting for his release. Sarah was now perceived as a pirate's wife, an associate to an outlaw and she was a disgraced fallen socialite. Her good standing now diminished, she was a single parent and alone. Perhaps she thought of her life up to now—twenty-nine-years-old, thrice married—she had gone from being the wife of two merchants to the wife of an accused pirate. Not even thirty years old and she had already lived a full life.

Sarah and Captain Kidd tried to figure out a way to get him out of prison. They asked Elizabeth Morris to go to Captain Thomas Clark's warehouse in Connecticut and retrieve a sack of gold Kidd had secretly given him in June when he was hovering around Gardiner's Island.[43] It was believed that Clark was holding £8000 of Kidd's money. That amount would work nicely as a bribe to a jailer. But Kidd's longtime friend refused to give Elizabeth any of the loot. He had already been arrested once by Lord Bellomont and he was afraid the Governor would do it again and maybe this time it would not be a temporary condition. He did not want to end up in prison like Kidd. Instead of helping Kidd, Clark betrayed him, delivering all of Kidd's goods to the governor but only on the condition that it was confirmed Kidd was in irons on a prison ship to England. Clark was afraid Kidd would retaliate for his double-crossing him if he was ever freed.[44]

Under Massachusetts law, Kidd could not be condemned to death for piracy, but the authorities wanted justice. They had sent the *Rochester* from London to take Kidd and the other imprisoned pirates back to London to stand trial. The ship was crippled in a storm and forced to turn around. The Admiralty immediately ordered a replacement and the HMS *Advice* was dispatched. Captain Wynn of the Royal Navy was in charge and given special orders pertaining to Kidd; he was to be in isolation so that he could not receive or give information. If anything leaked out from Kidd it would jeopardize the reputations of those high-ranking authorities that had sponsored his privateering voyage. By keeping Kidd quiet, the authorities attempted to hush any potential political scandal.

Discouraged but not disconsolate about the fact that Elizabeth Morris was not successful in getting his gold from Clark, Kidd continued to work on an escape plan. One version directly involved Sarah who was to sweet talk the jailor into allowing Kidd out of his chains. The other was for Kidd to use his personal charm to persuade the jailor to take off the cold irons that had been fastened to his ankle and wrists for months. It is uncertain which plan worked but the jailor took off the irons on Wednesday, Feb 8, 1699, out of compassion for Kidd's aching bones. The next step was for Sarah to figure out either how to loosen the bars so Kidd could slip by, or to use the old fashioned method—get the guards drunk so she could open the cell door. There was no time to spare because the HMS *Advice* had arrived in Boston's harbor.

The Kidds planned an escape for five days hence—February 13th—but they still had to figure out how to do it. Could Sarah get a gun into Kidd, or a knife or a file? Or could Kidd persuade the jailor, now a compassionate soul, to allow Sarah and Kidd a private visit together—it had been months since they had seen each other—and together they could plan the getaway?

The days were so cold there was ice on the harbor. Judge Samuel Sewell recorded in his diary that the days were the coldest in Boston's recent history.[45] Lord Bellomont was anxious to get the prisoners out of the prison and onto the king's ship so he would not have to deal with them any longer. But the weather made it impossible: a quick shift in temperature melted the ice, briefly unleashing a huge iceberg more than several hundred feet long, and it rammed into the *Advice*, eventually beaching it. Captain Cyprian Southack (who eighteen years later would be sent by the Governor to retrieve pirate treasure from the *Whydah*) and other mariners in Boston finally were able to right the ship and ferry it out to deep water in the harbor.

Kidd had been out of shackles five days, since February 8th, but Sarah had not been able to figure out a way to get her husband out of his cell. Lord Bellomont, weary from his poor health and distrustful of Captain Kidd, sent a man to check on Kidd. When he learned that Kidd was unshackled and moving about his cell, Lord Bellomont immediately demanded Kidd be re-shackled and set the date of the HMS *Advice's* departure for February 16th. Lord Bellomont did his planning in secret and the only men who were in on the plan were those who would transport the prisoners out of the prison to the harbor's edge and then row them five miles to the waiting ship. Lord Bellomont was not present when his men unlocked Kidd's cell, unshackled him and forced him out of the prison, so he did not see the skirmish that resulted when Kidd fought the men, or hear the tough words that were probably exchanged.

It had been seven months since Kidd had smelled fresh air. He and the other prisoners were tied up and taken to the HMS *Advice*. Once again Kidd was put in isolation and chained. By the time

Sarah awoke at the inn her husband was gone from prison. The door to his cell probably left open, the stench from his small space lingered in the air. Kidd had spent a total of eight months in Boston prison without being charged of a crime.

But the HMS *Advice* did not sail immediately. There were repairs to be made to the rigging and sails, more prisoners to load, food to store and, lastly, Kidd's treasure to load, which Lord Bellomont had collected from various people including John Gardiner and Captain Thomas Clark. John Gardiner's accounting of Kidd's treasure is detailed and every item from the buried treasure chest to the Goa stones and the silk quilts with tassels were turned over to Lord Bellomont. Gardiner also turned over the stolen loot he was holding for some of Kidd's men. Kidd's treasure was loaded onto his ship, the *Saint Antonio*, and his ship was sailed out to the HMS *Advice* where the loot was transferred under careful guard to the cargo area.

Captain Kidd was held prisoner on the HMS *Advice* in Boston harbor for three weeks. Captain Wynn made daily trips to the governor's mansion to stay apprised of the trip plans. Sarah sought out Captain Wynn and introduced herself. She then asked him if she could get a message to her husband — she wanted to say goodbye and send him her love. Sometime during the last eight months she and her husband had decided that she and the children would remain in America if he were taken to London. Kidd wanted to have them safe and he did not want them to see him in disgrace in Newgate prison in London. Captain Wynn insisted that he could not deliver a message to Kidd because he was under heavy guard. Sarah pressed a heavy gold ring in Captain Wynn's hand.[46] He said he could not accept gifts and tried to give her back the ring. She asked that he be kind to her husband and that he could keep the ring as a "token" until he brings her husband back to her.[47]

On March 10, 1700, the HMS *Advice* set sail for London carrying Captain Kidd, James Gilliam and thirty other pirates, mostly members of Kidd's crew. Captain Kidd was not treated like the other prisoners who were in chains in the gunroom: he was confined in a cabin in steerage. He arrived in London Sunday afternoon April 14, 1700 and was directed by the High Court of Admiralty to go aboard the yacht *Katherine* where he was to be escorted to Newgate prison, a five-story stone building on the corner of Newgate and Holborn Street in London. Shackled at the ankles and wrists, again he was put in solitary confinement in a cold, dank, putrid smelling cell that measured just fifteen feet by twenty feet and had a wooden platform for a bed. The Marshall who was watching over Kidd relayed to the Admiralty that Captain Kidd gave him a piece of gold and asked him to send it to his wife.[48] Kidd believed he was going to die since his papers were gone and he wanted to make one last effort to take care of her. The French passes Emott gave to Lord Bellomont "disappeared" and were not available as evidence of Kidd's innocence. Kidd asked that he not suffer the shameful death of hanging but instead be shot or given a knife, which the Marshall refused to do.[49]

Captain Kidd sat in Newgate prison for over a year before he was tried. During that time, even though he had not been tried and convicted they treated him like he was, not allowing him to have clean clothes, exercise, visitors or access to writing utensils. From the confinement he became very ill, suffering from pains in his head, fits, and other disorders of body and mind. The amenities were later granted, but only because the authorities thought he might die before his trial. In May 1700 he was allowed a visit by Mrs. Hawkins in the presence of a jail keeper.[50] Mrs. Hawkins was a distant relative of Sarah Kidd and she had been his landlady in 1695 when Kidd went to London to meet with some of the most powerful men in England to obtain a privateering license. So much had changed for Kidd since he last saw Mrs. Hawkins: now he was accused of piracy and murder and imprisoned in the disgusting Newgate prison. Mrs. Hawkins asked that he be allowed his trunk of fresh clothes. Her request was granted and she devotedly cared for him while he was sick.[51]

While Kidd languished in Newgate he tried to help the wives of two of his deceased crewmen, Henry Mead and William Beck, who had died in Madagascar five years before at the start of his privateering voyage. In keeping with the pirate's articles the personal effects of the men were sold at the mast to the highest bidder. Captain Kidd held the money from the auction for the wives but Lord Bellomont seized it when he was arrested. Captain Kidd sent Mrs. Hawkins' husband, Matthew Hawkins, to find the widows in London. After much effort, Elizabeth Mead and Gertrude Beck, accompanied by their lawyer, were finally given permission to visit Kidd at Newgate.

Kidd explained the situation to the women and told them he would try to help them get their money from the Admiralty. This was important news to Elizabeth Meade who was on the verge of going to debtors' prison for the unpaid bill of £10 her husband accumulated in New York before he left for sea.[52] Captain Kidd gave them the details of the case: where and how the men had died, and the list of the personal effects that were sold. For Henry Mead, the well-dressed, well-read first mate on Kidd's ship, Kidd had received 900 pieces of eight in gold for his personal effects. The inventory of his high-class good taste reads like that of an English gentleman than a seedy pirate: "brandy, tobacco, sea charts, mathematical books and instruments, twenty other books, six new suits of clothes, very good linen and bedding, five light-colored wigs, three pair of silver shoe buckles, two sets of silver buttons for sleeves, with stones in them, three hats and a good quantity of sugar."[53] William Beck had similar cargo and Captain Kidd received 450 pieces of eight in gold for his effects. The widows petitioned the Admiralty for their husbands' money but were refused. They petitioned directly to the king and were told that their request was read to King William but the king said he did not have the power to grant them their money and that they had to apply through the proper courts. Elizabeth Mead found a lawyer to press her claim in the High Court of Admiralty. She lost the case and it is highly likely that she went to debtor's prison.[54]

———⇒●◀———

Captain Kidd's trial finally took place on May 8 and 9, 1701. The trial was highly sensationalized and closely followed on both sides of the Atlantic. Many have questioned the fairness of the trial, and some legal experts think there was insufficient evidence to convict him. Others believe he was caught in the middle of the political warfare between the Tories and the Whigs and was used as political scapegoat to save the reputations of his prominent sponsors. Regardless, he was found guilty and sentenced to hang according to Admiralty custom at Execution Dock on the River Thames in London on May 23, 1701.

The fifty-six-year-old Scotsman had put up a hard fight defending himself at trial and presenting to the Admiralty Court numerous documents he had written explaining why he had done what he had done and contradicting the accusations against him. Before he was hanged, Captain Kidd again proclaimed his innocence and told those around him to send his love to his wife and daughters. He said his greatest regret "... was the thought of his wife's sorrow at his shameful death."[55] After Kidd had been tied up to the gallows, the rope broke and he fell to the ground. Disoriented but alive, he was immediately tied up again. This time, the rope held and he was hanged. His body was left in chains on display for many years as a gruesome reminder of the power of the colonial authorities.

Meanwhile, Sarah waited anxiously for news of her husband's innocence. She was sure he would return to her and that they would resume their happy life on Pearl Street. Instead, she got only his last words and news of his death. She received a warrant in August 1701 confiscating Kidd's estate. Sarah and the girls were forced to move out of the Pearl Street mansion and Sarah's properties and personal belongings were seized. Sarah hired an attorney and fought for what was rightfully hers, arguing that the properties and household furnishings were not Captain Kidd's, they were hers from her inheritance from William Cox. For two years, Sarah, little Sarah and Elizabeth lived quietly, keeping a very low profile. Then, in 1703, at the age of thirty-three, Sarah began her life again, marrying a New Jersey merchant named Christopher Rousby who was twenty years her senior. They had three sons and they named the last one William, perhaps in memory of Captain Kidd. Sarah and Rousby fought to regain her inheritance from William Cox and in 1704 Queen Anne granted her back the title to her Pearl Street mansion and all the other properties and money that had been tied up in legal bureaucracy for most of her adult life.

Sarah lived a long and eventful life but her will does not give a hint about it. She even protected the paternity of her two daughters with Kidd by identifying them in her will by their married names Sarah Latham and Elizabeth Troup. There are no photos of Sarah and all we have are a few documents, but there is one lasting image: by the end of her life in 1744, she could do more than scratch her initials, she could write her full name.

When people think of Captain Kidd, many remember him as a pirate who secretly buried treasure on Gardiner's Island. This is true, but only one side of the story. The other side of the story is about Captain Kidd the husband, father, and friend. In this version he is not a murderer and "America's most notorious pirate," he is a "gentleman" and was labeled so on his marriage license to his only wife, Sarah, because he was such a highly respected member of his New York community.

Kidd's story consists of a tapestry of relationships that weave together to bring to light the human side of a political manhunt. Numerous people on both sides of the Atlantic, especially in the New England communities of Rhode Island and Massachusetts, tried to help Captain Kidd escape his fate. His relationship with these people ranged from acquaintances to close family and friends. He had loyal friends who were willing to help him when he needed them. He had Mary and Edward Sands, who provided shelter for Sarah on Block Island and joined in the reunion on his sloop. He had his long time friend and lawyer James Emott. He had Duncan Campbell, at whose house the Kidds stayed when they were in Boston. He had John Gardiner, who safeguarded his treasure on Gardiner's Island. Mrs. Hawkins in England stepped up to help when he and Sarah's brother, Samuel Jr., needed a place to stay for six months in 1695, and five years later she took care of him when he was sick in Newgate prison. Matthew Hawkins helped Kidd locate the wives of two of his deceased crewmembers so he could do the right thing and help them get the money that was due to them. When Captain Kidd was a man on the run from the law, these people took a risk in associating with him. No one wavered. These were not fair weather friends; these were real relationships based on trust and loyalty; relationships the authorities claimed pirates did not have and were incapable of having because they were monsters. These relationships included women and the authorities claimed women were not a part of a pirate's world.

Sarah was the woman behind the man. Catapulted from the role of a wealthy New York socialite to a pirate's wife and an accomplice to a man on the run from the law, Sarah Kidd staunchly stood by the man she loved. Unable to write her name, she scratched her initials "SK" with purpose and conviction in black ink on early eighteenth-century documents showing respectful audacity. Fearlessly, she challenged the colonial authorities for what she believed was right. Perhaps unaware, or just unimpressed by the enormity of the political scandal that embroiled her and Captain Kidd for several years, she stood steadfast while the drama unfolded spanning two continents—the old world of London and the new world of colonial Boston. As a pirate's wife, she helped bring to the forefront the real story of Captain Kidd that involved secrets, lies, deceit, and betrayal. Her alliance and allegiance to her husband, as well as the support from his friends, is the unforgettable story of Captain Kidd that must be told.

CHAPTER 4

Window into the Private Lives of Pirates

Captain Samuel Burgess

Sarah Horne learned from Captain Samuel Burgess that he would be leaving New York soon on the *Margaret* to bring supplies to the pirates at Sainte-Marie Island near Madagascar. If she would like to send a letter to her husband, Jacob, who was a crewmember on Captain Kidd's *Adventure Galley*, he would keep her letter safe in his sea chest and deliver it to the pirates' "post office" on Ascension Island. The pirates had a well-organized mail system that made it possible for pirates, especially married pirates, to remain in touch with their families. Letters to and from the men on Madagascar and the islands were given to captains of trading vessels, then, on the return voyage, the same captain carried the replies.

Captain Burgess himself was a married former pirate with a better-than-average education who worked for the shrewd Manhattan merchant and ship owner Frederick Philipse. Philipse avoided the Navigation Acts by sending ships halfway around the world to exploit a multi-business operation with the rich Madagascar pirates. Burgess's assignment was to deliver sought-after provisions—Madeira wine, rum, salt, bread, sugar and lime juice (to prevent scurvy), calico, sewing notions, shoes, hats, brushes, combs, tobacco paper, various kinds of knives and hatchets to the pirate settlement and on the return trip bring back Madagascan slaves he acquired by trading munitions and pirate loot with local African kings.[1] Burgess provided a one-way shuttle service to the colonies for retiring Madagascar pirates. Men who had had enough of the pirate life and wanted to return to eighteenth century society paid their 100 pieces of eight and were ferried back to the colonies.[2]

On December 11, 1699, Burgess was on the return trip from Madagascar to New York when hubris and bad luck brought him to the attention of the authorities at the Cape of Good Hope. His visit there was only supposed to be a brief layover because he had a stop to make at Ascension Island at the pirates' post office and he had to load his deck with green turtles that lived in abundance on the island to have food for the long voyage home. Captain Mathew Lowth, a privateer with instructions from the Crown to capture pirates, had not planned on being in the harbor but bad weather delayed his trip three days. When Burgess sailed into the harbor in the *Margaret* flying the St. George's Cross of an English merchant ship, Lowth saluted him from his East India company ship. Burgess did not return the salute; he kept sailing to the Dutch fort and saluted the vessels there.

Lowth did not cotton to Burgess's insolence. He was so incensed he noted the insult in his logbook: "He took no manner of notice of me notwithstanding I had ye King's Jack and Pendant flying."[3] And then he took action: he seized the *Margaret*, arrested Burgess for trading with pirates and took into custody his crew and cargo of 114 slaves, twenty-eight pirates carrying their retirement money and the proceeds from the Sainte-Marie provision sale. In total £11,140 in coins and bullion was seized—a very large sum of money.[4] But the handsome fortune was not the real treasure—that was in Burgess's sea chest which contained Sarah Horne's letter and a handful of other personal letters to and from the pirates to their wives and family members. Fortunately for modern historians, the seizure happened so quickly Burgess did not have time to throw his sea chest overboard. Lowth turned the correspondence over to the Admiralty when he returned to London with his prize capture.

The sheer existence of the letters dispels the notion that pirates were illiterate social isolates estranged from land-based society. The letters show that correspondence was conducted tens of thousands of miles across the globe between Indian Ocean pirates and North American colonists and that there was successful and direct communication between New York and Madagascar and back again. The letters are plain paper folded and sealed with red wax. There are no envelopes or street addresses, only a simple instruction to the pirates' extensive world wide network to deliver the letter to "Thomas Pringle's wife in New York," or "To her Deare Loving husband Richard Wilday Aboard adventure Galle att Madagascar Or elsewhere." The letters from the wives show the difficulties of being apart from their husband. Left alone to care for the children and manage a family budget with no regular wages, the women tried to stay connected with their husbands across land and sea despite the long lapses in communication and the uncertainty of their circumstances. Their writing is conversational, newsy and sentimental, testifying to the loyalty and devotion of these wives determined to keep their marriage and family together. Their letters read as if they are leaving a note on the kitchen table for their husband to read when he comes home from work—only they did not know when or if he will return.

Sarah Horne wrote to her "Dear Dear Jacob Horne" from Flushing, New York June 5, 1698. Jacob Horne was a member of Captain Kidd's crew. She informed him that per his request she placed their son in an apprenticeship with a cousin, Isack Tayler. She brought him up to date with news of their friends and family and she mentioned that she had sent two letters to him before this one and received one from him confirming that the Ascension Island low-tech mail system worked. The harbors were popular hubs where information to and from the pirates was transmitted. Sarah's "flying news" about him more than likely came from the pirates returning from Madagascar. This letter shows the closeness of the maritime community; everyone knew each other and stayed in touch. Signing it "your true and faithful wife until death" Sarah addressed the outside of her love letter "For Jacob Horne on Board of Capt Kidd at Madagascar or elsewhere."[5]

My Dear Dear Jacob Horne this with my
Kind Love and harty Respects Rembered
To you Hoping to God that this few Lines
Will find you In Good Body health as....
They Leave me att this present time prays
Bee God for it

Deare Jacob having oportunyty I was willing to
Imbrace It and let you hear How It is with me
And your children they are well Margret presents

Her Duty to you your son I have put out according
To your Desire to our Couson Isack Tayler tell
You come home again pray Bee so kind If
You have opertunity as to Lett us hear from
You If possible how It is with you all for
Wee here abundance of flying news concerning
You when for I should bee very Glad to hear
From you-but Glader If it should please
God that I should your face one more
Oure Relations and friends are all well
And give theyr loves to you I have sent you
Two letters before this and have Received
One no more att present But giving my prayers
To ye Almyty for your Helth and happiness so I
Rest your true and faithfull wife till Death

Denis Holdren and wife are
Alive and well & Remembers
Theyr kind love to you and
Theyr Dear Son willing

Sarah Horne

The sea chest on Burgess' ship had letters that included information about bequests left by pirates for their wives and families. Pirates' had last wills and testaments and powers of attorney documents. These were form letters filled in with names, dates and details. Samuel Burgess was clearly an important colleague to his fellow pirates because several of them named him executor of their estates in their wills and a few even gave him power of attorney. It was commonly believed and promoted by the authorities that pirates lived outside the law, but these documents show that the pirates and their families adhered to conventional Anglo-American legal and social norms.

The letter of Elizabeth Breho shows the difficulty wives faced trying to obtain their late husband's estate. Not only were there middlemen involved but also the long distance time lag of the pirates' mail system made the outcome of success less likely. Elizabeth Breho, the wife of pirate William Breho, wrote from Newport, Rhode Island on May 23, 1698 to pirate Elias Rowse in Madagascar demanding that her husband's money be returned to her because she had learned of his death and knew Rowse held all his estate. She had already taken the proper legal steps for this resolution by giving Samuel Burgess power of attorney so that Rowse could deliver the money to Burgess. She implored him to have the character of an honest man and she hoped he would honestly and faithfully perform the will of the deceased to his widow.

Rowse wrote on Breho's actual letter a note to John Dodd asking him to deliver to Samuel Burgess 400 pieces of eight. In a separate letter to Mrs. Breho nearly a year later Rowse replied that he had sent the money home with John Dodd almost three years previously because he was going home to New York City and he knew her husband wanted the money delivered to her at the first opportunity. Elias Rowse said he had not gone home to Mattatanna so he sent the money through the pirate system where the next available pirate traveling to New York would deliver it to the pirate's widow in Newport, Rhode Island. It is not known if she ever received her inheritance. It is highly unlikely since it had been three years and Brother Dodd had not delivered the money. Elizabeth Breho's letter is written in her own hand. Elias Rowse addressed the outside of the letter to "To Mrs. Eliz Beeho in Newport Rhode Island:"[6]

> *Elias Rowse Sr I understanding By Captain Molton*
> *That att My Husband William Breho His deth you …*
> *Pleased to take care of what is left by him & Having the*
> *Carrecter of an Honest Mnh, Depon With Confidence I …*
> *My opinion yr designe is Not to Wrong of Widdow & the*
> *Father … this oppertum*
>
> *…*
>
> *Bear Mr. Samuel Burgess*
> *Unto whom I have give a letter of Attorney with power*
> *To deliver of … for the same … I hope*
> *You will honestly & faithfully performe will of deceased*
> *To his widow … take*

My leave of ... remain your friend and servant to command

Eliz Breho

Elias then responded to Eliz:

Brother John Dodd I would desire
You would be so kind to deliver onto
Capt Sam Burgess 400 peces of 8/8 belonging
To ye widow Breho and in so doing you will oblidge your
Friend and servant to command

Elias Rowse

Another letter from Elias to Eliz regarding the estate:

April ye 19th 1699
Mrs. Breho I have received your but
Ye money is not in my hands for I
Delivered ye money to John Dodd
Almost 3 years ago by reason he
Was going home your husband desiring
To send iff ye first opportunity
But I have ... not gone home
But is non at Mattatanna ... is
All at present from your friend
And servant to Command

Elias Rowse

Captain Evan Jones wrote to his "Honored Father" from the *Peter*, a ship he stole after natives burned his ship, the *Beckford Galley*. He informed him that since he left England he had endured great hardship losing his ship but he managed to save 900 pounds for each man and that he is now captain of his small vessel. He told his father he would not hear from him for about five years. He sent love to his sisters, brothers, uncle and other relations. Captain Jones wrote a similar letter to his wife Frances, who lived in Gramorganshire near Cardiff South Wales.[7]

Honored Father
Having now this opportunity of writing to you

By the way of New York this is to satisfy you that
I am at present att St. Laurencs an Island in the
East Indies and one of the Greatest in the ...
I have endured a great deal of hardships since
My last departure ut of England I have been
Forced this 5 months to run ... by
... of ... of ... at last I
got to be ... and then I
fortune but fortune was very unkind for I lost
the ship but by God providence saved all our goods
and ... all saved about 900 pound a man in money I am att
present chapn. Of a small vessel so I have given
you an amount of my life since you last heard
from me I ... you shall not hear from me
again this 5 years more at present but my
duty to you and love to brothers and sisters and
... to my unkle y all y rest of my
relations from your Dutyfull son

Evan Jones
November 4th, 1698
From off the Ship
Peter riding in Augustine
Bay on the Island off St. Laurence

Burgess's misstep at the Cape of Good Hope was a boon for pirate enthusiasts because it shed light on the private world of pirates and their wives and families. Captain Lowth hauled Burgess off to London where he was thrown in jail, put on trial for piracy, found guilty and sentenced to hang. Burgess was not only an employee of Frederick Philipse, he was related through marriage to Philipse's only niece.[8] Philipse helped secure Burgess' release on bail and several months later he was granted the King's pardon.[9] Upon gaining his freedom, he became involved in various maritime enterprises and he visited his wife and children at their New York home. In 1708 he returned to his old stomping ground in Madagascar where he returned to piracy and dealing in the slave trade with local African kings. He lived a rootless life for another several years until he died in 1716 at the age of sixty-six from poisoning by a local African king.[10] The reason for the violence against him is unclear but it may have been related to a dispute over a business arrangement involving slaves. A fellow pirate converted his belongings to cash and the money was delivered via the pirate Indo-Atlantic network to his wife in New York.[11]

Conclusion

Richard Caverley was in charge of navigation and sailing on Paulsgrave Williams' ship, and Jeremiah Higgins was the boatswain, in charge of all deck activities including regularly inspecting the rigging and sails. Next to the quartermaster, these two were the most important members of the crew. But piracy was not for them. They had been on ships sailing out of Jamaica for the Spanish wrecks on the coast of Florida when their vessels were captured by the pirates and forced against their will to join the crew.[1] At the first opportunity, they wanted to escape to save themselves from the wrath of the authorities.

It was June 1717, shortly after Paulsgrave Williams had stopped at Block Island to visit his mother and sister. Williams was off the coast of New York in the *Marianne* and he was desperately in need of water for his crew. While he was in a discussion with another ship captain, Caverley and Higgins jumped ship and an elaborate manhunt took place throughout New England looking for the runaway pirates. The two men were caught, imprisoned in irons and brought to trial. "The Piracy Trial of 1717," heard by the Vice Admiralty Court of New York, was one of the largest piracy trials of the colonial period. Twenty-eight depositions were taken, including two from women. The large number of depositions reflects the determination of His Majesty's Council to rid the seas of pirates.

The irony of the authorities' efforts to stop pirates and bring them to justice is that the depositions actually served to humanize them because the depositions showed the community and resources in place to help the pirates. The authorities scoured the area looking for information and even deposed a butcher who gave a dish of lamb to one of the pirates. But the most important testimony came from Elizabeth Byfield and Catherine Dobbs who provided shelter and safety to the pirates. The court's demand for the women's testimony shows that it was well known that women associated with pirates.

Elizabeth Byfield ran a rooming house in New York City and she gave Jeremiah Higgins a pillow, blanket, and a room.[2] It is unclear from her one-paragraph testimony if she knew Higgins was a pirate but it is certain that her house was a well-known destination for mariners in need, otherwise she would not have answered her door at midnight like she did. Higgins stayed at the Byfield house for several days until he was captured. He was carrying a large amount of gold and silver that he testified was his share of the booty for the last two and a half years, and some was payment for his injury incurred during an attack on a French ship under the command of Samuel Bellamy.[3]

Catherine Dobbs and her husband, William, let Richard Caverley stay at their house for a few hours. He told them his life was in danger and he had to escape from the area. Catherine hid Caverley at her brother's house, who lived on a nearby island. Several times she rowed out to the island in her boat and carried back Caverley's letters and gold to a ship captain—Captain Vincent—willing to help him escape.

While Caverley and Higgins waited in prison, news of the King's pardon arrived and they were released as part of the General Pardon in 1718. Catherine Dobbs and Elizabeth Byfield were not charged as accomplices, and were allowed to go free. The authorities claimed women played little or no part in a pirate's world except as prostitutes or tavern maids. The testimonies of Elizabeth Byfield and Catherine Dobbs show that these women were neither prostitutes nor tavern maids. They were merely women in a maritime community willing to help other mariners.

It has been more than three hundred years since pirates walked the docks of Atlantic seaports, careened their vessels in hidden island alcoves, and hoisted their dreaded black flag, but still the men who wreaked havoc on international trade during the Golden Age of Piracy continue to capture our imagination. Researchers have published scores of scholarly books and creative artists have produced hundreds of novels, plays, and movies about them. Yet, after all of this, the cultural image of pirates that has come down to us is one-dimensional. Whether they are portrayed as romantic outlaws who defied the convention of their society or as anti-social villains who were the "enemies of the human race," the common assumption about pirates is that they were radically individualistic and scornful of the common ties that bind society together. Young, unmarried, unemployed deep-water sailors from the lowest rungs of society, poor and uneducated, pirates were at best social isolates with no connection to society beyond the confines of the pirate ship, and at worst, violent monsters with no human decency. Until now, the description from the French historian Hubert Deschamps of pirates was taken as truth:

> ...a unique race, born of the sea and of a brutal dream, a free people, detached from other human societies and from the future, without children and without old people, without homes and without cemeteries, without hope but not without audacity, a people for whom atrocity was a career choice and death a certitude of the day after tomorrow.

But the general characterization of eighteenth-century pirates is wrong and women, family, and communities played a larger part in the lives of pirates than has been previously acknowledged. The stereotypes of pirates have become myths and I have discredited those myths with historical facts that cause us to significantly qualify the one-dimensional image of pirates.

There are several misrepresentations that I have sought to correct in this book, the first being that pirates were social isolates faithful only to their own men on the ship. Alexander Exquemelin, in his book *The Buccaneers of America*, made it clear that although the pirates had their own commonwealth on the wooden decks of the ship and on land in their pirate communities, it was not limited only to them. The ship's articles acknowledged that their fellow buccaneers had ties outside the confines of the ship and those ties were not only respected but the pirates supported those relationships by making provisions to provide for the wives, families, or friends of the deceased pirate.

We know also from primary source documents—letters, wills and power of attorney documents found on Captain Samuel Burgess's ship—that pirates were not social isolates. The pirates had an extensive network that kept them in touch with the outside world. They had a mail system that allowed communication between the pirates and their families and there was a commuter service from Madagascar to New York that made it possible for pirates who had had enough of the pirate life to return to society. This commuter service was available several times a year and twenty-eight retired pirates were on Captain Burgess's ship when it was captured. Lord Bellomont, Governor of New York, wrote to the Council of Trade and Plantations in London May 3, 1699, that he could not apprehend two or three pirates who he knew were in New York because they had returned home to their wives and families. Bellomont acknowledged that the pirates were not social isolates, that they often had standing in their community and that the community protected the pirates from the authorities. He wrote, "I laid out for 'em, but they are too well befriended to be given up to justice."[4] The large network of family and friends that Captain Kidd had on both sides of the Atlantic Ocean also challenges the assumption that pirates were social isolates. The authorities had it wrong: not all pirates were social isolates without a country and a home.

Another misrepresentation is that the pirates were labeled arch villains by colonial authorities, "enemies of the human race." By calling pirates villains, they demonized them, denying them the full range of their humanity. There was more to the men than just violence and greed, and the authorities knew that, but to consider the pirates as men rather than monsters would have compromised their collective efforts to stop piracy. Take the example of Captain William Kidd. Captain Kidd gave gifts to Mrs. John Gardiner and Mrs. Duncan Campbell as a gesture of his appreciation for what they did for him, and he sent his wife Sarah his last piece of gold from his prison cell in London while he awaited his trial. His last words were love for his wife and daughter and regret at "the thought of his wife's sorrow at this shameful death." These are not the actions and words of a monster. If the pirates were inhuman and uncivilized beasts, why did they have such strong rules of governance and civility in their ship's articles that included, among other things, a health insurance plan for the injured and a life insurance plan (of sorts) for the families and relations of dead pirates? If all pirate captains were so uncivilized, why did Samuel Bellamy have the nickname "The Pirate Prince"? The authorities intentionally did not present a fair assessment of pirates in order to support and embellish their propaganda campaign against the sea robbers and deliberately created the myth that pirates were arch villains.

Yet another misrepresentation that was widely promoted by the authorities was the notion that pirates were unmarried men. This is not true. My archival research has uncovered at least eighty married pirates out of the several hundred who are mentioned on crew lists, depositions, trial records, letters from families, wills, last words, power of attorney documents, newspaper articles, letters from the colonial authorities published in the *Calendar of State Papers Colonial, America and West Indies* series for the period 1680–1730, and literature from the late seventeenth century to the present. Captains Samuel Burgess, Evan Jones, William Kidd, Thomas Paine, Andrew Knott, James Gilliam and Paulsgrave Williams were all married. Some had married men in their crews. Captain Bellamy is not able to be included among the married men because of his early death, but as we know, he was likely returning to Cape Cod to wed Maria Hallett. The specific mention in the ship's articles of not taking married men proves that pirates were married and had to join a ship where married men were allowed. Many pirates embraced the social norm of marriage.

Another way that pirate life was misrepresented was the belief that pirates did not have families. Captain Kidd had his wife Sarah, daughters Sarah and Elizabeth, and his uncle in England. Paulsgrave Williams was especially close with his mother and three sisters and separated from Captain Bellamy and the pirate flotilla to visit them on Block Island. Paulsgrave Williams' extended family played an important role in the political and economic life of early New England, especially Block Island. Many pirates did have family, and they maintained meaningful relationships with them.

It was widely believed that pirates lived in a male-centered world and that women played little part in their lives. This is simply not true. It was commonly thought women were not a part of a pirates' world because pirates were perceived to be among the toughest and most vicious members of a heavily masculinized seafaring culture whose cruelty and violence set them apart from normal human beings. But there can be no disputing the fact that despite the great challenges of their dangerous occupation, their prolonged time at sea and unpredictable location because of the roving nature of their business, many pirates still maintained relationships with their wives, families, and communities on land.

There was a network of women who helped Captain Kidd—his wife, Sarah, his extended family of Mrs. Hawkins and Paulsgrave Williams' two sisters—Mary and Elizabeth. A common thread among these women, even in disparate locations—New York, Block Island, Boston and London—was care and concern for Captain Kidd. The story of Captain Samuel "Black Sam" Bellamy would not be the same without the legend of his lover Maria Hallett.

Captain Paulsgrave Williams's family brought to light female agency in the man's world of piracy. Piracy provided opportunities for the indirect participation of women, which varied according to the needs and nature of the seafaring community. It is clear that female participation was encouraged and it facilitated piratical activity. Williams's sisters were actively involved in the pirate business and loyal friends to the pirate Captain Kidd and his wife Sarah.

For the period 1695–1742, women's names are on petitions, letters, and court documents from pirates' wives, families, and communities and makes clear the extent to which women were involved with them. If they were really such brutal monsters, why did they have wives and families back home trying desperately to maintain contact with them, and petitioning for their release when they were jailed? The women in the petitions were strong and bold and sought approval from the highest power—from Queen Anne in the case of the Madagascar wives and relations; from the Governor and Council in the case of Sarah Kidd and from the High Court of Admiralty in the case of Elizabeth Meade and Gertrude Beck. For each of these women, their plea for assistance was their last resort. There were clear-cut laws about what to do with pirates, but the laws were ambiguous or not even written about when it came to a pirate's family because the colonial authorities did not even acknowledge them. History was written by men back then, and pirates' wives and children are rarely mentioned in trial records and confessions of pirates. From London to Boston, the women and kin of pirates were in need of a special kind understanding to remedy their extraordinary and unfortunate circumstance.

The handful of letters to and from Madagascar found in Captain Burgess's mailbag show the consequences of the long-distance relationship common to the maritime culture. The uncertainty, the insecurity, the heartfelt sense of loss of missing loved ones contradict the cynical colonial authorities' denial of the pirates' deep connections and relationships on land. The letters from the pirates to their wives or relations are appropriate coming from a husband or son, so that it is hard to describe the authors as the "savage beasts" the authorities painted them to be.

"The Piracy Trial of 1717" shows the short-term relationships of women with pirates and way pirates needed women who provided them with lodging, transportation and a convenient cover for their visits on shore. The women's depositions brought voiceless women into pirate history. One day they are minding their own business acting in partnership with their husbands, going about their daily chores, and the next day they are involved with a runaway pirate and testifying before the Admiralty Court in New York. It is unclear if this was the first time Catherine Dobbs and Elizabeth Byfield came into contact with pirates, but their eager willingness to support and assist them hints that they had done this before. Their collusion with piratical enterprise reaffirms the fact that women were needed as the pirates' agents on land. A pirate's domain was the sea. He was a misfit and an outlaw on land and needed direction as to where to go for the basic necessities of food and shelter. In some cases, women collaborated with the pirates for economic reasons only. Elizabeth Byfield was in a business relationship with Jeremiah Higgins, offering him a room to rent. But it is unclear if there were economic benefits for Catherine Dobbs; she showed a strong tendency to nurture and protect Richard Caverley despite the risks to herself and her husband.

Except for Sarah Kidd, very little is known about these women. They are just names in history, but they are important because they validate pirates as men who had lives that intersected with others. They are also an invaluable resource because they make visible through a name and date the women who have been thus far invisible in history. Now women are a part of pirate literature in the Golden Age.

Captain Charles Johnson's popular book, *The General History of the Pyrates* discussed in detail the "otherness" of pirates as outlaws or outcasts, living beyond the pale of civil and commercial society, whose relationships with women bordered on lurid fantasy.[5] Although my sample size is small, the discussion of women in the chapters of the four pirate captains—Bellamy, Williams, Kidd, and Burgess—and the petitions, letters and depositions in "The Piracy Trial of 1717" do not hint of "lurid fantasy." Instead, they contradict this harsh and narrow description of pirates and their relationships with women. There is no question that the relationships were not perfect: Captain Williams abandoned his wife and children, Samuel Burgess died in Madagascar away from his wife and children in New York, and Captain Kidd had been away from his wife and daughters for three years before they were reunited near Block Island. The realities of maritime life meant separation of distance and time, straining many relationships as was seen in the petitions and some of the letters asking the pirate to send news of his well being.

The expansion of trade in the West Indies, West Africa and North America created opportunities and problems for women. There was the potential for riches if the pirate survived and returned home with his plunder, but there was also the risk of abandonment and death. When pirates were on land, women were engaged in making contacts for them or assisting in negotiations on their behalf. The common thread that runs through this book about women is that of their strength and practicality. For most of the women, they had to survive alone in a relationship that was full of uncertainty. What is important to realize is that there were relationships between pirates and wives, families, and communities. There are histories, petitions, letters and depositions to prove it.

Another way pirates have been misrepresented is that they were portrayed as illiterate. Captain Kidd defended himself in his trial in London and trial records show his beautiful handwriting and his strong arguments for his defense. Richard Caverley was also literate. He penned a letter to Captain Vincent asking for help escaping the authorities by taking him "to sea in his sloop."[6] And we know Captain Samuel Burgess could read and write because a letter found in the mailbag from his employer, Frederick Philipse, was addressed to him. The seven-page letter detailed the tasks of the voyage and mentions correspondence he received from Captain Burgess. Also, there was Captain Evan Jones' letter in the mailbag addressed to his father.

The final misrepresentation is that pirates were from the lowest rung of society. While this is largely true, it is not entirely true and the authorities had an interest in making this over-generalization. Captain Paulsgrave Williams, for example, is a clear exception to this claim. He was not a former sailor but a trained goldsmith before he turned pirate. He came from a highly educated and wealthy Rhode Island family. His was a family of doctors and civil servants and his father had been the Attorney General of Rhode Island. Paulsgrave Williams was far from the lowest rungs of society; he was from a distinguished high-class family. Not all pirates were poorly educated former sailors from the lowest rungs of society.

This book has challenged the stereotype of an eighteenth-century pirate and argued that pirates must be viewed through a wider lens to include their wives, families, and communities. If the authorities had included the pirates' private sphere in the literature it would have conveyed a very different public impression of the men they loved to hate. Not all pirates were "enemies of the human race." They were also husbands, fathers, sons, brothers and friends.

This book has an inherent emphasis on human values—on the concern for others and the thought processes and actions that reflect that concern. It has focused on a particular group of human beings—pirates—who have been misrepresented in the historiographical and popular literature and have continued to be misunderstood as something other than human. It has examined how human values in the broadest and best sense extended into the community and the world of pirates in a way that has hitherto not been explored, by focusing on the pirates' relationships with their wives, families, and communities. That focus has allowed us to see these men as three-dimensional human beings who had feelings and concerns like all human beings do.

Of course pirates were not engaged in an honorable profession, nor have I portrayed them that way. There is no question that these men were thieves—and in the case of Samuel Bellamy, he was one of the best in the business—but embedded in lives devoted to thievery was a distinct and variously-layered moral code evident both in the man-to-man contracts and, even more so, in their relations with the women, families, and communities devoted to them. What I intended to do was to portray pirates in a more realistic and humanistic light—as ordinary men who exhibited the full range of capabilities, both positive and negative. Examining them through the lens of human values brought to light the serious flaw in the traditional image of pirates and proves that the claim that they were the "enemies of the human race" is simply not accurate.

This historical study of pirates, framed in the past and with a focus on human value, provides new insights showing that pirates were not simply dark figures; they were a mixture of bad and good. In some situations, the evidence reveals that there was an extensive gray area in which these men dwelled. Pirate or privateer? Privateer or pirate? Examining these men through the lens of their relationships with their wives, families, and communities brings out a unique understanding of pirates as part of a larger human drama. In this book they are subject to the same ethnical considerations as those who sought to imprison them. They were not monsters who roamed the high seas but individuals who sought to live their lives under difficult and challenging circumstances. No one could say it better than Captain Edward Low, who was reported by the authorities to be one of the most vile and vicious of the pirates. In speaking to his crewmembers he said, "Tho' we are Pirates, yet we are Men, and tho' we are deem'd by some People dishonest, yet let us not wholly divest ourselves of Humanity, and make ourselves more Savage than Brutes."[7]

Notes

Introduction

Abbreviations:
ADM—Admiralty Paper
CO—Colonial Office Paper
HCA—High Court of Admiralty Papers
PRO—Public Record Office

1. Hubert Jules Deschamps, *Les Pirates á Madagascar* (Paris: Berger-Levrault, 1972) quoted in Richard Zacks, *The Pirate Hunter* (New York: Hyperion Books), 41.

2. Robert C. Ritchie, "Samuel Burgess, Pirate," in *Authority and Resistance in Early New York*, eds. William Pencak and Conrad Edick Wright (New York: New York Historical Society, 1988), 131.

3. Daphne Palmer Geanacopoulos, "Discovering Cape Cod's Unknown Subculture: A Social Narrative Based on the Artifacts from the Pirate Ship *Whydah*." (Master's Thesis Georgetown University, May 2007), 7.

4. Marcus Rediker, *Villains of all Nations: Atlantic Pirates in the Golden Age* (Boston: Beacon Press, 2004), 87.

5. CO 323/6, no. 81, PRO.

6. Rediker, *Villains of all Nations*, 10.

7. David Cordingly, *Spanish Gold* (London: Bloomsbury, 2011), 8.

8. George Francis Dow and John Henry Edmonds, *The Pirates of the New England Coast 1630–1730* (New York: Dover Publications, 1996), 228.

9. Alexander O. Exquemelin, translated by Alexis Brown, *The Buccaneers of America* (Harmondsworth, England: Penguin Books Ltd., Reprint, Mineola, New York: Dover Publications, 2000), 53–54; Joel H. Baer, "The Complicated Plot of Piracy: Aspects of English Criminal Law and the Image of the Pirate in Defoe," *The Eighteenth Century* 23, no. 1 (Winter 1982): 23.

10. Historians Robert C. Ritchie and Hans Turley, have suggested that pirates lived in a male-only homosexual world, but they bring forward little evidence in support of their assertions. I do not think the partnership of two pirates in the contract of matelotage was necessarily a partnership between two gay men.

11. Exquemelin, *The Buccaneers of America*, 53–54.

12. Kenneth J. Kinkor, interview by author by phone, March 1, 2006, McLean, Virginia.

13. Malcolm Cowley, "The Sea Jacobins," *The New Republic*, February 1, 1933, 329.

14. Peter Earle, *The Pirate Wars* (New York: Thomas Dunne Books, 2003), 164.

15. Rediker, *Villains of all Nations*, 68.

16. Exquemelin, *The Buccaneers of America*, 70–71.

17. Ibid.

18. Ibid., 72.

19. Joel H. Baer, ed., *British Piracy in the Golden Age: History and Interpretation, 1660–1730* (London: Pickering and Chatto, 2007), vol.1:xxxiv.

20. Ibid., 13.

21. Captain Charles Johnson, *A General History of the Pyrates*, ed. by Manual Schonhorn (London: J.M. Dent & Sons, 1972, reprint, New York: Dover Publication, 1999), 6.

22. Colin Woodward, "The Last Days of Blackbeard," *Smithsonian* (February 2014): 34–36.

23. Dow and Edmonds, *The Pirates of the New England Coast*, 201.

24. Ibid., 142.

25. Ibid., 227.

Chapter 1

1. Erick Ekholm and James Deetz, "Wellfleet Tavern," *American Museum of Natural History*, September 1971, 56.

2. Daphne Palmer Geanacopoulos "Well, Some Pirates Were Art Lovers, Too" *New York Times*, April 24, 2002.

3. Kenneth J. Kinkor, interview by author by phone, April 7, 2013, McLean, Virginia.

4. Elizabeth Reynard, *The Narrow Land: Folk Chronicles of Old Cape Cod* (Chatham, Massachusetts: Chatham Historical Society, 1978), 214–229.

5. Ibid., 214.

6. Kenneth J. Kinkor, interview by author, April 4, 2012, at the Whydah Museum in Provincetown, Massachusetts.

7. Reynard, *The Narrow Land*, 215.

8. Ibid.

9. Kenneth J. Kinkor, ed. *The Whydah Sourcebook 2006*, (unpublished manuscript used with permission by the editor), "Last Will and Testament of Mary Hallett," Barnstable County Public Record Vol. 8., April 19, 1734, 284.

10. Kinkor, *Sourcebook*, 324.

11. Last Will and Testament of Mary Hallett, April 19, 1734.

12. Ibid.

13. Kinkor, *Sourcebook*, 324.

14. Ibid., 338.

15. Ibid.

16. Kenneth J. Kinkor, interview by author, April 4, 2012, at the Whydah Museum in Provincetown, Massachusetts.

17. Kinkor, *Sourcebook,* 104.

18. Kenneth J. Kinkor, interview by author, April 4, 2012, at the Whydah Museum in Provincetown, Massachusetts.

19. Arthur T. Vanderbilt II, *Treasure Wreck: The Fortunes and the Fate of the Pirate Ship Whydah* (Boston: Houghton Mifflin, 1986), 14.

20. Ibid., 15.

21. Ibid.

22. Marcus Rediker, *Between the Devil and the Deep Blue Sea,* "The Seaman as Pirate" (Cambridge: Cambridge University Press, 1987), 256.

23. Vanderbilt, *Treasure Wreck,* 15.

24. Ibid., 39.

25. Donald G. Shomette, *Pirates on the Chesapeake: Being a True History of Pirates, Picaroons, and Raiders on Chesapeake Bay 1610–1807* (Centerville, Maryland: Tidewater Publishers, 1985), 184.

26. Rediker, *Villains of all Nations,* 33.

27. Barry Clifford and Paul Perry, *Expedition* Whydah (New York: Harper Collins, 1999), 168.

28. Vanderbilt, *Treasure Wreck,* 17.

29. Kinkor, *Sourcebook,* 342.

30. Ibid., 342–345.

31. The Substance of the Examination of John Brown in "The Tryal of Eight Pirates at Boston." May 6, 1717 in Kinkor, *Sourcebook,* 112.

32. Matt Woolsey, "Top-Earning Pirates" *Forbes* Magazine, September 19, 2008.

33. Rediker, *Villains of all Nations,* 33.

34. Deposition of Abijah Savage, Commander of the Sloop *Bonetta* of Antigua before His Excellency Walter Hamilton, Antigua, 30 November 1716, CO Papers 137/11, no. 45iii in Kinkor, *Sourcebook,* 78–79.

35. Clifford and Perry, *Expedition Whydah,* 225.

36. Ibid.

37. Kenneth J. Kinkor, interview by author, April 4, 2012, at the Whydah Museum in Provincetown, Massachusetts.

38. The Substance of the Examination of John Brown in "The Tryal of Eight Pirates at Boston." May 6, 1717 in Kinkor, *Sourcebook,* 112.

39. Ibid.

40. Clifford and Perry, *Expedition Whydah,* 252.

41. Ibid., 251.

42. The Substance of the Examination of Peter Hoof in "The Tryal of Eight Pirates at Boston." May 6, 1717 in Kinkor, *Sourcebook,* 116.

43. Kenneth J. Kinkor, interview by author by phone, February 26, 2006, McLean, Virginia.

44. The Substance of the Examination of John Brown at "The Tryal of Eight Pirates at Boston." May 6, 1717 in Kinkor, *Sourcebook*, 112.

45. Ibid.

46. Kinkor, *Sourcebook*, 209.

47. The Substance of the Examination of John Shuan at "The Tryal of Eight Pirates at Boston." May 6, 1717 in Kinkor, *Sourcebook*, 116.

48. Exquemelin, *The Buccaneers of America*, 73.

49. Clifford and Perry, *Expedition Whydah, 253.*

50. Johnson, *The General History of the Pyrates, 587.*

51. Clifford and Perry, *Expedition Whydah*, 255.

52. Kinkor, *Sourcebook*, 305.

53. Rediker, *Villians of All Nations*, 32.

54. Shomette, *Pirates on the Chesapeake*, 187.

55. Ibid.

56. Kenneth J. Kinkor, interview by author by phone, February 26, 2006, McLean, Virginia.

57. Deposition of Thomas Fitzgerald & Alexander Mackonochie, Boston. May 6, 1717 in John Franklin Jameson, ed. *Privateering and Piracy in the Colonial Period: Illustrative Documents, #109* (Gloucester, United Kingdom: Dodo Press, 2008), 339–340.

58. Dow and Edmonds, *Pirates of the New England Coast,* 127.

59. Ibid.

60. Barry Clifford, interview by author by phone, February 6, 2006, McLean, Virginia.

61. "Deposition of Ralph Merry and Samuel Roberts: Boston. May 11 and May 16, 1717" in Jameson, *Privateering and Piracy, #111*, 345–346.

62. Ibid.

63. Barry Clifford and Peter Turchi, *The Pirate Prince: Discovering the Priceless Treasurers of the Sunken Ship Whydah* (New York: Simon & Shuster, 1993), 28.

64. Ibid.

65. Ibid.

66. "The Tryal of Eight Pirates at Boston." October 22, 1717 in Kinkor, *Sourcebook*, 190.

67. Ibid.

68. Ibid.

69. Dow and Edmonds, *Pirates of the New England Coast,* 123.

70. "Deposition of Thomas Fitzgerald & Alexander Mackonochie" Boston. May 6, 1717 in Jameson, *Privateering and Piracy*, #109, 340.

71. Ibid.

72. Clifford and Perry, *Expedition Whydah, 263.*

73. "The Tryal of Eight Pirates at Boston." October 22, 1717 in Kinkor, *Sourcebook*, 191.

74. Ibid.

75. Ibid.

76. Kinkor, *Sourcebook*, 329.

77. Dow and Edmonds, *Pirates of the New England Coast*, 124.

78. Kinkor, *Sourcebook*, 330.

79. Ibid.

80. Clifford and Perry, *Expedition Whydah*, 264.

81. Reynard, *The Narrow Land*, 221.

82. Ibid., 223.

Chapter 2

1. Kenneth J. Kinkor, interview by author by phone, April 7, 2013, McLean, Virginia.

2. Alexander Boyd Hawes, *Off Soundings Aspects of the Maritime History of Rhode Island* (Chevy Chase, MD: Posterity Press, 1999), 49.

3. Kenneth J. Kinkor, interview by author by phone, April 7, 2013, McLean, Virginia.

4. "Examination of Jeremiah Higgins" New York, June 22, 1717, Vice Admiralty Court of New York in Kinkor, *Sourcebook*, 150.

5. Deposition of John Lucas, Master of the Ship *Tyral* of Brighthelmstone of Great Britain before John Hart, Governor of Maryland. Annapolis. 13 April 1717. Colonial Office Papers 5/1318 no. 16iii, in Kinkor, *Sourcebook*, 90.

6. Burgess and Fiske, *New Shoreham Town Record Book I, from dates 1666–1717*, Manuscript transcription, 1924, 40.

7. Samuel Truesdale Livermore, *A History of Block Island: From Its Discovery, In 1514, To the Present Time, 1876* (Hartford: The Case, Lockwood & Brainard Co., 1877), 237; Burgess and Fiske, *New Shoreham Town Book I, 112.*

8. Temple Prime, *Descent of Comfort Sands and of his Children*, with notes on the families of Ray, Thomas, Guthrie, Alcock, Palgrave, Cornell, Dodge, Hunt, Jessup (New York: The DeVinne Press, 1886), 8.

9. Kenneth J. Kinkor interview by author, April 4, 2012, at the Whydah Museum Provincetown, Massachusetts.

10. Samuel Truesdale Livermore, *The History of Block Island: From Its Discovery, In 1514, to The Present Time, 1876,* (Hartford: The Case, Lockwood & Brainard Co., 1877), 268.

11. Rhode Island Historical Preservation Commission, "Historical and Architectural Resources of Block Island, Rhode Island," 5.

12. Last Will and Testament of Anna Guthrie in New Shoreham, Block Island. Town Clerk's Office.

13. G. Andrews Moriarty, "The Alcocks of Roxbury, Massachusetts," *The New England Historical and Genealogical Register*, Jan. 1943, 10–14.

14. Michelle Marchetti Coughlin, *One Colonial Woman's World The Life and Writings of Mehetabel Chandler Coit* (Boston: University of Massachusetts Press, 2012), 28.

15. G. Andrews Moriarty, "Some Notes on Block Islanders of the Seventeenth Century" in *New England Historical Genealogical Register* Jan–Dec. (Boston: New England Historical Genealogical Society, 1951), 163.

16. Articles of Agreement on the Contract of Marriage Between Anna Alcock and John Williams January 25, 1669/70 is on pages 62–65 in "*Descent of Comfort Sands and of this Children.*" Also in Suffolk Deeds, Lib. VI, Suffolk County, Massachusetts sections 165, 166, 241, 242, and 243. The date of her prenuptial agreement is January 25, 1669. It is possible they were married on that date.

17. G. Andrews Moriarty, "Some Notes on Block Islanders of the Seventeenth Century," *New England Historical Genealogical Register* Jan–Dec. (Boston: New England Historical Genealogical Society, 1951), 178.

18. Kenneth J. Kinkor interview by author by phone, April 7, 2013, McLean, Virginia; Colin Woodward, *The Republic of Pirates* (New York: Harcourt, 2007), 96; Barry Clifford, *The Lost Fleet* (New York: Harper-Collins, 2002), 108–118, 262–264.

19. John Osborne Austin, *Genealogical Dictionary of Rhode Island; Comprising three Generations of Settlers who Came Before 1690*, (Baltimore: Genealogical Publishing Co., 1969), 223.

20. Moriarty, "Some Notes on Block Islanders of the Seventeenth Century," in *New England Historical Genealogical* Register Jan–Dec. (Boston: New England Historical Genealogical Society, 1951), 174; Malcolm Sands Wilson, *Descendants of James Sands of Block Island*, (New York: Privately printed, 1949), 85.

21. Colin Woodward, *The Republic of Pirates*, (New York: Harcourt, 2007), 179.

22. Moriarty, "Some Notes on Block Islanders of the Seventeenth Century," 174.

23. Woodward, *The Republic of Pirates*, 96.

24. Last Will and Testament of Anna Guthrie, December 12, 1718.

25. Newport Town Council Records 1728–1775 in the archives of the Newport Historical Society, Newport, Rhode Island, 206.

26. G. Andrews Moriarty, "Abigail Williams," in *Genealogies of Rhode Island Families* Vol. II (Baltimore: Genealogical Publishing Co.: 1983), 405.

27. "Rhode Island Dispatch of May 3, 1717" *Boston News-Letter* May 6, 1717.

28. Woodward, *The Republic of Pirates*, 179.

29. Records of the Vice-Admiralty Court of the Province of New York 1685–1838 in Kinkor, *Sourcebook*, 147–148.

30. Hawes, *Off Soundings*, 54.

31. Woodward, *The Republic of Pirates*, 193.

32. Barry Clifford and Peter Turchi, *The Pirate Prince: Discovering the Priceless Treasurers of the Sunken Ship Whydah* (New York: Simon & Shuster, 1993), 72.

33. Dow and Edmonds, *The Pirates of the New England Coast*, 131.

34. Clifford and Turchi, *The Pirate Prince*, 72.

35. Dow and Edmonds, *Pirates of the New England Coast*, 125.

36. Woodward, *The Republic of Pirates*, 54.

37. Boston *News-Letter*, May 20, 1717.

38. Woodward, *The Republic of Pirates*, 193.

39. "Boston Notice, May 27, 1717," Boston *News-Letter* in Kinkor, *Sourcebook*, 135.

40. "Deposition of Samuel Skinner," Salem, MA. May 26, 1717, Suffolk Court files in the Massachusetts Archives, folio no. 11945, in Kinkor, *Sourcebook*, 138.

41. Dow and Edmonds, *The Pirates of the New England Coast*, 345.

42. William Snelgrave, *A New Account of Some Parts of Guinea and the Slave Trade, Part III*, (London: James, John & Paul Knapton, 1734), 216–217, 257–259.

43. The specifics of the death of Paulsgrave Williams are not known other than it is thought that he drowned. This information is in the *Letter Book of Peleg Sanford*, Providence: Rhode Island Historical Society, 1928), p. 35, n. 83.

Chapter 3

1. Berthold Fernow, Ed., *Calendar of Wills, 1626–1836* (New York: Knockerbocker Press, 1896), 318.

2. Alice Morse Earle, *Colonial Days in Old New York* (New York: Charles Scribner's Sons, 1896 reissued by Singing Tree Press, Detroit, Michigan, 1968), 102–103.

3. Alexander Winston. *No Man Knows My Grave* (Boston: Houghton Mifflin, 1969), 114.

4. Richard Zacks, *The Pirate Hunter* (New York: Hyperion Books: 2002), 86.

5. CO 5:860, no. 64 XXV, PRO.

6. Williard Hallam Bonner, "Clamors and False Stories" the Reputation of Captain Kidd, *The New England Quarterly*, vol. 17, no. 2 (June, 1944): 180.

7. CO 5:860, no. 64 XXV, PRO.

8. Ibid.

9. Ibid.

10. David Cordingly, *Under the Black Flag* (New York: Random House, 1995), 183.

11. CO 5:860, no. 64 XXV, PRO.

12. CO 5:860, no. 64, PRO. "Examination of Gabriel Loffe."

13. C.O. 5:860, no. 64 XXV, PRO.

14. HCA l/98 f. 128 PRO. "Letter from Lord Bellomont to Captain Kidd," New York, June 8, 1698.

15. *Calendar of State Papers Colonial, America and West Indies* #680 xi, July 6, 1699.

16. Frederic de Peyster, *The Life and Administration of Richard, Earl of Bellomont, Governor of the Provinces of New York* (New York: New York Historical Society, 1879), 29.

17. CO 5:860, no. 64 XXI, PRO. Footnote to the "Narrative of John Gardiner," July 17, 1699 in Jameson, *Privateering and Piracy*, 251.

18. Harold T. Wilkins, *Captain Kidd and his Skeleton Island* (New York: Liveright Publishing Corporation, 1937), 141. "Statement by Duncan Campbell to Governor Bellomont."

19. *Calendar of State Papers Colonial, America and West Indies,* #746 XIX Boston, "Deposition of Captain Kidd," September 4, 1699.

20. Ibid.

21. CO 5:860, no. 64 XXI, PRO. "Narrative of John Gardiner," in Jameson, *Privateering and Piracy in the Colonial Period*, 251.

22. Ibid.

23. Robert C. Ritchie, *Captain Kidd and the War Against the Pirates* (Cambridge, Massachusetts: Harvard University Press, 1986), 230.

24. Wilkins, *Captain Kidd and his Skeleton Island*, 289.

25. Dunbar Maury Hinrichs, *The Fateful Voyage of Captain Kidd* (New York: Bookman Associates, Inc., 1955), 131.

26. Wilkins, *Captain Kidd and his Skeleton Island*, 141.

27. *Calendar of State Papers Colonial, America and West Indies* # 680 XXIV, "Examination of Captain Kidd before the Governor and Council," July 3, 1699.

28. *Calendar of State Papers Colonial, America and West Indies* #680, "Letter from Lord Bellomont to the Board of Trade," July 26, 1699.

29. Ibid.

30. CO 5:860, no. 64 Commons Journal, XIII 19–21 in Jameson in *Privateering and Piracy in the Colonial Period*, 257, "Lord Bellomont to the Board of Trade," July 26, 1699.

31. *Calendar of State Papers Colonial, America and West Indies* #680, "Letter to Lord Bellomont to the Board of Trade," July 26, 1699.

32. Massachusetts Archives, Boston, Massachusetts, 62, no. 316.

33. Hawes, *Off Soundings*, 15.

34. Richard Zacks, *The Pirate Hunter* (New York: Hyperion, 2002), 232.

35. *Calendar of State Papers Colonial, America and West Indies* #1011, "Governor the Earl of Bellomont to the Council of Trade and Plantations," November 29, 1699.

36. CO 5:861, no. 4 XVIII, PRO also in Jameson, *Privateering and Piracy in the Colonial Period*, 255. "Sarah Kidd to Thomas Payne," July 18, 1699.

37. Ibid.

38. CO 5:861, no. 4, PRO "Lord Bellomont to the Board of Trade," November 29, 1699 in Jameson, *Privateering and Piracy in the Colonial Period*, 269.

39. Wilkins, *Captain Kidd and his Skeleton Island*, 138; Zacks, *The Pirate Hunter*, 264.

40. Wilkins, *Captain Kidd and his Skeleton Island*, 140.

41. Massachusetts Archives, Vol. 61, no. 317, July 25, 1699 "Petition of Sarah Kidd."

42. Zacks, *The Pirate Hunter*, 275.

43. Ibid.

44. Ibid., 276.

45. Ibid., 278.

46. Ibid., 286.

47. Ibid.

48. Wilkins, *Captain Kidd and his Skeleton Island*, 184.

49. Ibid.

50. Ritchie, *Captain Kidd*, 200, 224.

51. Zacks, *The Pirate Hunter*, 96.

52. Ibid., 340.

53. Ibid., 341.

54. Ibid.

55. Ibid., 392.

Chapter 4

1. HCA 1/98 f. 85 PRO. Captain Samuel Burgess's Cargo list of the *Margaret*.

2. HCA 1/98 f. 42 PRO. "Deposition of Captain Samuel Burgess," March, 1699.

3. Robert C. Ritchie, "Samuel Burgess, Pirate," in *Authority and Resistance in Early New York*, eds. William Pencak and Conrad Edick Wright (New York: New York Historical Society, 1988), 119.

4. Zacks, *The Pirate Hunter*, 306; Ritchie, "Samuel Burgess, Pirate," in *Authority and Resistance in Early New York*, 125.

5. HCA 1/98 ff. 118–119 PRO.

6. HCA 1/98 ff. 110, 175 PRO.

7. HCA 1/98 ff. 183, 184 PRO.

8. F. D. Arnold-Forster, *The Madagascar Pirates* (New York: Lothrop, Lee and Shepard Co., 1957), 62.

9. Jacob Judd, "Frederick Philipse and the Madagascar Trade," *New York Historical Society Quarterly* 55, no. 4 (1971): 372.

10. John C. Appleby, *Women and English Piracy 1540–1720* (Woodbridge, UK: The Boydell Press, 2013), 34–36.

11. Don C. Seitz, *Under the Black Flag Exploits of the Most Notorious Pirates* (New York: Dover Publications, 2002), 71–75.

Conclusion

1. "Examination of Jeremiah Higgins" New York. June 22, 1717. Vice Admiralty Court of New York, in Kinkor, *Sourcebook*, 150; "Examination of Richard Caverley," June 15, 1717, Vice Admiralty Court of New York in Kinkor, *Sourcebook*, 148.

2. "Examination of Elizabeth Byfield," June 15, 1717, Vice Admiralty Court of New York: "Piracy Case of 1717."

3. "Examination of Jeremiah Higgins" New York. June 22, 1717. Vice Admiralty Court of New York in Kinkor, *Sourcebook*, 150.

4. *Calendar of State Papers Colonial Series*, #343, "Governor the Earl of Bellomont to Council of Trade and Plantations," May 3, 1699.

5. Ibid., 122.

6. "Examination of Catherine Dobbs" June 15, 1717 Vice Admiralty Court of New York.

7. Dow and Edmonds, *The Pirates of the New England Coast,* 191.

Bibliography

Andrews, C.M. *Guide to the Materials for American History, to 1783, in the Public Record Office of Great Britain*. Vol. II Departmental and Miscellaneous Papers. Washington, D.C.: Carnegie Institution of Washington 1914.

Andrews, William L. Sargent Bush, Jr., Annette Kolodny, Amy Schrager Lang and Daniel B. Shea, eds. *Journeys in New Worlds Early American Women's Narratives*. Madison: The University of Wisconsin Press, 1990.

Appleby, John. *Women and English Piracy, 1540–1720*. Woodbridge, UK: The Boydell Press, 2013.

Arnold-Forster, F. D. *The Madagascar Pirates*. New York: Lothrop, Lee and Shepard Company, 1957.

Austin, John Osborne. *The Genealogical Dictionary of Rhode Island; Comprising Three Generations of Settlers Who Came Before 1690, With Many Families Carried to the Fourth Generation*. Baltimore: Genealogical Publishing Company, 1969.

Baer, Joel H. ed. *British Piracy in the Golden Age: History and Interpretation, 1660–1730, Vols 1–4*. London: Pickering and Chatto, 2007.

_____. "Penelope Aubin and the Pirates of Madagascar: Biographical Notes and Documents." In *Eighteenth-Century Women: Studies in their Lives, Work and Culture, Volume I*, ed. Linda V. Troost, 49–62. New York: AMS Press, 2001.

_____. " 'The Complicated Plot of Piracy': Aspects of English Criminal Law and the Image of the Pirate in Defoe." *The Eighteenth Century* 23, no. 1 (Winter 1982): 3–26.

Bailyn, Bernard. *The New England Merchants in the Seventeenth Century*. Cambridge: Harvard University Press, 1979.

Bartlett, John Russell, ed. *Records of the Colony of Rhode Island, and Providence Plantations, in New England* Vol. III 1678 to 1706. Providence: Knowles, Anthony & Co., State Printers, 1858.

Berkin, Carol. *First Generations Women in Colonial America.* New York: Hill and Wang, 1996.

Berkin, Carol, and Leslie Horowitz, eds. *Women's Voices, Women's Lives.* Boston: Northeastern University Press, 1998.

Bolster, W. Jeffrey. *Black Jacks: African American Seamen in the Age of Sail.* Cambridge: Harvard University Press, 1997.

Bonner, William Hallam. *Pirate Laureate: The Life & Legends of Captain Kidd.* New Brunswick, NJ: Rutgers University Press, 1947.

Bowen, Richard LeBaron. *Rhode Island Colonial Money and its Counterfeiting 1647–1726.* Concord, New Hampshire: The Rumford Press, 1942.

Bridenbaugh, Carl. *Fat Mutton and Liberty of Conscience Society in Rhode Island, 1636–1690.* Providence: Brown University Press, 1974.

Brigham, Albert Perry. "Cape Cod and the Old Colony." *Geographical Review.* 10, no. l: (July, 1020): 1–22. Journal online. Available at http://www.jstor.org/stable/207274. Accessed 29 March 2010.

Brunell, Kathleen. *Bellamy's Bride.* Charleston: The History Press, 2010.

Bunker, Nick. *Making Haste from Babylon; The Mayflower Pilgrims and Their World A New History.* New York: Alfred A. Knopf, 2010.

Burg, B.R. "Legitimacy and Authority: A Case Study of Pirate Commanders in the Seventeenth and Eighteenth Centuries." *The American Neptune: A quarterly Journal of Maritime History* 34, no. 1 (January 1977): 40–49.

Channing, Edward. *A History of the United States Volume II A Century of Colonial History 1660–1760.* New York: The Macmillan Company, 1908.

Chapin, H.M. "Captain Paine of Cajacet," in *Rhode Island Historical Society Collections* (Jan. 1930), 23: 20.

Clarke, Hermann F. "John Hull: Mintmaster." *The New England Quarterly,* 10, no. 4 (Dec., 1937): 668–684. Journal online.

Available from http://www.jstor.org/stable/359931. Accessed 10 November 2010.

Clifford, Barry L., and Paul Perry. *Expedition Whydah*. New York: Harper Collins, 1999.

Clifford, Barry L., and Peter Turchi. *The Pirate Prince*. New York: Simon and Shuster, 1993.

Cordingly, David. *Under the Black Flag*. New York: Random House, 1995.

_____. *Spanish Gold*. London: Bloomsbury, 2011.

Coughlin, Michelle Marchetti. *One Colonial Woman's World: The Life and Writings of Mehetabel Chandler Coit*. Boston: University of Massachusetts Press, 2012.

Cowley, Malcolm. "The Sea Jacobins," *The New Republic*. 1 February 1933.

Coyle, John G., Edmund J. Mcguire, and Vincent J. O'Reilly, eds. *The Journal of the American Irish Historical Society, Vol. XVIII*. New York: Published by the American Irish Historical Society, 1919.

Crane, Elaine Forman. *Ebb Tide in New England Women, Seaports and Social Change, 1630–1800*. Boston: Northeastern University Press, 1998.

Creighton, Margaret S., and Lisa Norling. *Iron Men, Wooden Women: Gender and Seafaring in the Atlantic World, 1700–1920*. Baltimore: Johns Hopkins University Press, 1996.

Dayton, Cornelia Hughes. *Women Before the Bar Gender Law & Society in Connecticut, 1639–1789*. Chapel Hill: University of North Carolina Press, 1995.

Defoe, Daniel. *Five Novels Complete and Unabridged*, "Captain Singleton." Barnes & Noble, Inc.: New York, 2007.

De Peyster, Frederic. *The Life and Administration of Richard, Earl of Bellomont, Governor of the Provinces of New York*. New York: New York Historical Society, 1879.

Demos, John. *A Little Commonwealth Family Life in Plymouth Colony*. Oxford: Oxford University Press, 1970.

_____, ed. *Remarkable Providences 1600–1760*. New York: George Braziller, Inc., 1972.

Dorman, Margaret Scoville. "Legend and Literature of Captain William Kidd." *Connecticut Magazine*, vol. 1 (1905): 269–279.

Dow, George Francis, and John Henry Edmonds. *The Pirates of the New England Coast 1630–1730*. New York: Dover Publications, 1996.

Drake, Samuel Adams. *Nooks and Corners of the New England Coast*. Westminster, MD: Heritage Books, 2008. Originally printed by Harper & Brothers, 1874.

Earle, Alice Morse. *Colonial Days in Old New York*. Detroit: Singing Tree Press, 1968.

Earle, Peter. *The Pirate Wars*. New York: Thomas Dunne Books, 2003.

Exquemelin, Alexander O. Translated by Alexis Brown. *The Buccaneers of America*. Harmondsworth, England: Penguin Books Ltd., 1969. Reprint, Mineola, New York: Dover Publications, 2000.

Faber, G.C. ed., *The Poetical Works of John Gay Including 'Polly' 'The Beggar's Opera' and Selection from the other Dramatic Work*. London: Oxford University Press, 1926.

Fernow, Berthold. *New York Colony Council Calendar of Council Minutes 1668–1783*. Harrison, New York: Harbor Hill Books, 1987.

Fiske, Jane Fletcher. *Gleanings from Newport Court Files 1659–1783*. Boxford, MA: Jane Fletcher Fiske self published, 1998.

_____. Indexer. *New Shoreham Town Book* 1684–1717, Vol.1. This is a transcribed Xeroxed copy of the original town records of New Shoreham, Block Island.

Forbes, Harriette Merrifield. *New England Diaries, 1602–1800: A descriptive Catalogue of Diaries, Orderly Books and Sea Journals*. Topsfield: Perkins Press, 1923.

Freeman, Frederick. *History of Cape Cod: Annals of Barnstable County*. General Books: 2009, originally published 1860.

Frey, Sylvia R., and Marian J. Morton. *New World, New Roles A Documentary History of Women in Pre-Industrial America*. New York: Greenwood Press, 1986.

Galvin, Peter. R. *Patterns of Pillage: Geography of Caribbean Based Piracy in Spanish America, 1536–1718*. New York: Peter Lang, 1999.

Geanacopoulos, Daphne Palmer. "Discovering Cape Cod's Unknown Subculture: A Social Narrative Based on the Artifacts from the Pirate Ship *Whydah*." Georgetown University Master's Thesis, May, 2007.

_____. "Eighteenth Century Piracy Through a Wider Lens: Recasting the Image of Pirates to Include their Wives, Families and Communities," Georgetown University Doctoral Thesis, 2014.

Gosse, Philip. *The History of Piracy*. New York: Dover Publications, 2007.

Hall, Michael Garibaldi. *Edward Randolph and the American Colonies 1676–1703*. New York: W.W. Norton & Company, 1960.

Harper, Lawrence A. *The English Navigation Laws A Seventeenth Century Experiment in Social Engineering*. New York: Columbia University Press, 1939.

Hawes, Alexander Boyd. *Off Soundings Aspects of the Maritime History of Rhode Island*. Chevy Chase, Maryland: Posterity Press, 1999.

Heyrman, Christine Leigh. *Commerce and Culture The Maritime Communities of Colonial Massachusetts 1690–1750*. New York: W.W. Norton & Company, 1984.

Hibbert, Christopher. *The Roots of Evil A Social History of Crime and Punishment*. Boston: Little, Brown and Company, 1963.

Hill, Christopher. *The World Turned Upside Down*. London: Penguin Books, 1972.

_____. "Radical Pirates?" In *The Collected Essays of Christopher Hill*, Vol. 3. Amherst: University of Massachusetts Press, 1986.

Hinrichs, Dunbar Maury. *The Fateful Voyage of Captain Kidd*. New York: Bookman Associates, 1955.

Hitchings, Sinclair. "Guarding the New England Coast: The Naval Career of Cyprian Southack." In *Seafaring In Colonial Massachusetts: Publications of the Colonial Society of Massachusetts*, Vol. 52, 43–65. Boston: University Press of Virginia, 1980.

Hodge, Christina J. "Widow Pratt's World of Goods: Implications of Consumer Choice in Colonial Newport, Rhode Island." *Early American Studies: An Interdisciplinary Journal* 8, no. 2, (Spring 2010): 217–234. Journal on-line. Available from http://muse.jhu.edu/login?uri=/journals/early_american_studies_an_

interdiscipliary_journal/v008/8.2.hudge01.pdf. Accessed 26 October 2010.

Hough, Charles Merrill, ed. *Reports of Cases in the Vice Admiralty of the Province of New York and in the Court of Admiralty of the State of New York 1715–1788*. New Haven: Yale University Press, 1925.

Hull, N.E.H. *Female Felons: Women and Serious Crime in Colonial Massachusetts*. Chicago: University of Illinois Press, 1987.

Innes, Stephen, ed. *Work and Labor in Early America*. Chapel Hill: The University of North Carolina Press, 1988.

James, Sydney V. *Colonial Rhode Island: a History*. New York: Charles Scribner's Sons, 1975.

Jameson, John Franklin, ed. *Privateering and Piracy in the Colonial Period: Illustrative Documents*. Gloucester, United Kingdom: Dodo Press, 2008.

Johnson, Charles. *A General History of the Pyrates*. Manuel Schonhorn, ed. London: J.M.Dent & Sons, 1972. Reprint, New York: Dover Publication, 1999.

Judd, Jacob. "Frederick Philipse and the Madagascar Trade." *New York Historical Society Quarterly*, 55, issue 4, (1971).

Kinkor, Kenneth J. "Black Men Under the Black Flag" in *Bandits at Sea: A Pirates Reader*. ed. C.R. Pennell, 200–208. New York: New York University Press, 2001.

_____, ed. "The *Whydah* Sourcebook 2006." Unpublished manuscript from the Whydah Museum, Provincetown, MA. Given to the author by the editor, Kenneth Kinkor.

Koehler, Lyle. *A Search for Power: The "Weaker Sex" in Seventeenth-Century New England*. Chicago: University of Illinois Press, 1980.

Konstam, Angus. *The World Atlas of Pirates*. Guilford, Connecticut: The Lyons Press, 2009.

Kritzler, Edward. *Jewish Pirates of the Caribbean*. New York: Anchor Books, 2008.

Leeson, Peter T., *The Invisible Hook: The Hidden Economics of Pirates*. Princeton: Princeton University Press, 2009.

Lemish, Jesse. "Jack Tar in the Streets: Merchant Seamen in the Politics of Revolutionary America." *The William and Mary Quarterly*, Third Series, 25, no. 3 (July, 1968): 371–407. Journal online. Available from http://www.jstor.org/stable/192 1773. Accessed: November 2011.

Little, Benerson. *The Sea Rover's Practice: Pirate Tactics and Techniques, 1630–1730.* Dullas, Virginia: Potomac Books, 2005.

Livermore, Samuel Truesdale. *A History of Block Island: From Its Discovery, In 1514, To the Present Time, 1876.* Hartford: The Case, Lockwood & Brainard Co., 1877.

Lockridge, Kenneth A. *Literacy in Colonial New England; And Enquiry into the Social Context of Literacy in the Early Modern West.* New York: W.W. Norton & Co, Inc., 1974.

Lydon, James G. *Pirates, Privateers, and Profits.* Upper Saddle River, NJ: The Gregg Press, 1970.

Mackie, Erin. *Rakes, Highwaymen, and Pirates, The Making of the Modern Gentleman in the Eighteenth Century.* Baltimore: The John Hopkins University Press, 2009.

Marley, David F. *Pirates of the Americas.* Santa Barbara: ABC-CLIO, 2010.

McDonald, Kevin P. *Pirates, Merchants, Settlers and Slaves: Making and Indo-Atlantic World, 1640–1730.* Ph.D. Dissertation in History. University of California, Santa Cruz. June 2008.

Meinig, D.W. "Atlantic America 1492–1800." *The Shaping of America: A Geographical Perspective on 500 years of History.* Vol. 1. New Haven: Yale University Press, 1986.

Merton, Robert K. "Insiders and Outsiders: A Chapter in the Sociology of Knowledge." *The American Journal of Sociology* 78, no. 1 (July 1972): pp. 9–47. Journal on-line. Available from http://www.jstor.org/stable/27776569. Accessed 27 January 2010.

Middleton, Richard, and Anne S. Lombard. *Colonial America: A History to 1763.* Chichester, West Sussex, U.K.: Wiley-Blackwell, 2011.

Mills, Barbara. *Providence 1630–1800 Women Are Part of Its History.* Bowie, Maryland: Heritage Books, 2002.

Morgan, Edmund S. *The Puritan Family Religion & Domestic Relations in Seventeenth Century New England.* Westport: Greenwood Press, 1966.

Moriarty, G. Andrews. "Some Notes on Block Islanders of the Seventeenth Century." In *New England Historical Genealogical*

Register (Jan–Dec.). Boston: New England Historical Genealogical Society, 1951.

_____. "Abigail Williams" in *Genealogies of Rhode Island Families* Vol. II. Baltimore: Genealogical Publishing Co. Inc., 1983. 404–406.

Morris, Richard B. *Government and Labor in Early America.* New York: Columbia University Press, 1946.

Norton, Mary Beth. *Founding Mothers & Fathers: Gendered Power in the Forming of American Society.* New York: Vintage Books, 1997.

O'Callaghan, E.B. ed. *Records Relating to the Colonial History of the State of New York.* Albany: Weed, Parsons and Company Public Printers, 1854.

_____. *The Documentary History of the State of New York* Vol. II Albany: Weed, Parsons and Company Public Printers, 1850.

Paine, Gustavus Swift. "Ungodly Carriages on Cape Cod." *The New England Quarterly* 25, no.2 (Jun., 1952): 181–198. Journal online. Available from http://www.jstor.org/stable/362161. Accessed 29 March 2010.

Palfrey, John Gorham. *The History of New England From the Revolution of the Seventeenth Century, Book IV.* Boston: Little, Brown, and Co., 1885.

Porter, Marilyn. "She was Skipper of the Shore-Crew: Notes on the History of the Sexual Division of Labour in Newfoundland." *Labour/LeTravail,* 15 (Spring, 1985): 105–123. Journal online. Available from http://www.jstor.org/stable/25140555. Accessed 22 November 2011.

Post, Jerrold M. *The Mind of the Terrorist: The Psychology of Terrorism from the IRA to al-Qaeda.* New York: Palgrave Macmillan, 2007.

Pratt, Enoch. *A Comprehensive History, Ecclesiastical and Civil, of Eastham, Wellfleet, and Orleans; County of Barnstable, Mass., From 1644–1844.* Originally published by W.S.Fisher and Co, 1844. General Books, 2009.

Preston, Diana and Michael. *A Pirate of Exquisite Mind: Explorer, Naturalist and Buccaneer The Life of William Dampier.* New York: Berkley Books, 2004.

Prime, Temple. *Descent of Comfort Sands and of His Children, With Notes on the Families of Ray, Thomas, Guthrie, Alcock,*

Palgrave, Cornell, Dodge, Hunt, Jessup. New York: The De Vinne Press, 1886.

Pringle, Patrick. *Jolly Roger: The Story of the Great Age of Piracy.* New York: Dover Publications, 2001.

Rediker, Marcus. "Under the Banner of King Death": The Social World of Angle-American Pirates, 1716–1726. *The William and Mary Quarterly,* Third Series, 38, no. 2 (Apr., 1981): 203–227. Journal on-line. Available from http://www.jstor.org/stable/1918775. Accessed 17 March 2010.

_____.*Villains of All Nations: Atlantic Pirates in the Golden Age.* Boston: Beacon Press, 2004.

Reynard, Elizabeth. *The Narrow Land: Folk Chronicles of Old Cape Cod.* Chatham: The Chatham Historical Society, 1934.

Rich, Shebnah. *Truro, Cape Cod: Or Land Marks and Sea Marks.* Boston: D. Lothrop and Company, 1884.

Ritchie, Robert C. *Captain Kidd and the War Against the Pirates.* Cambridge: Harvard University Press, 1986.

_____. "Kidd, William (c. 1645–1701)." In *Oxford Dictionary of National Biography*, edited by H.C.G. Mathew and Brian Harrison. Oxford: OUP, 2004. On-line ed., edited by Lawrence Goldman, October 2009. http://0-www.oxforddnb.com.library. lausys.georgetown.edu/view/article/15515 (accessed December 11, 2011).

_____. "Samuel Burgess, Pirate," in *Authority and Resistance in Early New York*, eds. William Pencak and Conrad Edick Wright. New York: New York Historical Society, 1988.

Robey, Richard C. ed. "Diary of Samuel Sewall 1674–1729." *Research Library of Colonial Americana.* I and II. New York: Arno Press, 1972.

Rogozin'ski, Jan. *Honor Among Thieves.* Mechanicsburg, PA: Stackpole Books, 2000.

Rushfort, Brett, and Paul W. Mapp. *Colonial North America and the Atlantic World: A History in Documents.* Upper Saddle River: Pearson Prentice Hall, 2009.

Salinger, Sharon V. *Taverns and Drinking in Early America.* Baltimore: The Johns Hopkins University Press, 2002.

Salmon, Marylynn. *Women and the Law of Property in Early America*. Chapel Hill: The University of North Carolina Press, 1986.

Sanford, Peleg. *The Letter Book of Peleg Sanford a Newport Merchant (Later governour of Rhode Island) 1666–1668*. Providence: Rhode Island Historical Society, 1928.

Schwartz, Amy D. "Colonial New England Agriculture: Old Visions, New Directions." *Agricultural History* 69, no. 3 (Summer, 1995): 454–481. Journal online. Available from http://www.jstor.org/stable/3744338. Accessed 27 October 27 2010.

Seitz, Don. C. ed. *The Tryal of William Kidd for Murder and Piracy*. New York: Dover Publications, 2001.

_____. *Under the Black Flag: Exploits of the Most Notorious Pirates*. New York: Dover Publications, 2002.

Senior, Clive. *A Nation of Pirates: English Piracy in its Heyday*. New York: Crane, Russak & Company, Inc., 1976.

Sewell, Samuel. *Diary of Samuel Sewall, 1674–1729*, Vol. II. New York: Arno Press, 1972.

Seybolt, Robert Francis, Jonathan Barlow and Nicholas Simons. "Captured by Pirates: Two diaries of 1724–1725." *The New England Quarterly* 2, no. 4 (Oct., 1929): 658–669. Journal online. Available from http://www.jstor.org/stable/359173. Accessed 14 November 2010.

Sheffield, William P. *A Historical Sketch of Block Island*. Newport: John P. Sanborn & Co, Mercury Office Printers, 1876.

_____. *An Address Delivered by William P. Sheffield Before The Rhode Island Historical Society, In Providence, February, 1882*. Newport: John P. Sanborn, Printer, 1883.

Smith, Merril D., ed. *Sex and Sexuality in Early America*. New York: New York University Press, 1998.

Snelgrave, William. *A New Account of Some Parts of Guinea, I. The History of the Late Conquest of the Kingdom of Whidaw by the King of Dahomè II. The Manner How the Negroes Become Slaves. III A Relation of the Author's Being Taken by Pirates*. London: James, John and Paul Knapton, 1734.

Snow, Edward Rowe. *Secrets of the North Atlantic Islands*. New York: Dodd Mead and Company, 1950.

_____. *Pirates and Buccaneers of the Atlantic Coast.* Beverly, Massachusetts: Commonwealth Editions, 1944.

Snow, Pamela J. "Increase and Vantage: Women, Cows, and the Agricultural Economy of Colonial New England." In *Women's Work in New England, 1620–1920.* ed. Peter Benes, 22–34. Boston: Boston University, 2001.

Soukhanov, Anne D. ed, *The American Heritage Dictionary, Third Edition.* Boston: Houghton Mifflin, 1996.

Stensrud, Rockwell. *Newport: A Lively Experiment 1639–1969.* Newport: Redwood Library and Athenaeum, 2006.

Stokes, I.N. Phelps. *The Iconography of Manhattan Island 1498–1909.* Vol. 1. Arno Press: New York, 1967.

Swift, Charles Francis. *Cape Cod, The Right Arm of Massachusetts: An Historical Narrative.* Yarmouth: Register Publishing Company, 1897.

Synenki, Alan T., and Sheila Charles. *Archeological Collections Management of the Great Island Tavern Site, Cape Cod National Seashore, Massachusetts.* Boston: Division of Cultural Resources North Atlantic Regional Office National Park Service U.S. Department of the Interior, 1984.

"The Rhode Island Historical Magazine." Vol. 3–4. (1882–1884). Newport: Newport Historical Publishing Co.

Tannenbaum, Rebecca J. *The Healer's Calling: Women and Medicine in Early New England.* Ithaca: Cornell University Press, 2002.

Thoreau, Henry David, and William F. Robinson. *Cape Cod.* Boston: Little Brown and Company, 1985.

Turley, Hans. *Rum, Sodomy and the Lash: Piracy, Sexuality and Masculine Identity.* New York: New York University Press, 1999.

Ulrich, Laurel Thatcher. "Women's Travail, Men's Labor: Birth Stories from Eighteenth-Century New England Diaries." In *Women's Work in New England, 1620–1920,* ed.Peter Benes, 170–184. Boston: Boston University, 2001.

_____. *Good Wives: Image and Reality in the Lives of Women in Northern New England 1650–1750.* New York: Vintage Books, 1991.

Vickers, Daniel. *Young Men and the Sea.* New Haven: Yale University Press, 2005.

_____. "Work and Life on the Fishing Periphery of Essex County, Massachusetts, 1630–1675."

Volo, Dorothy Denneen and James M. *Daily Life in The Age of Sail.* London: Greenwood Press, 2002.

Wall, Helena M. *Fierce Communion: Family and Community in Early America.* Cambridge: Harvard University Press, 1990.

Waters, Henry Fritz-Gilbert ed. *The New England Historical & Genealogical Register Vol.* VI. Boston: Thomas Prince, 1852.

Watson, W.L. "A Short History of Jamestown" in *Rhode Island Historical Society Collections* (April 1933), 26: 40.

Weeden, William B. *Economic and Social History of New England 1620–1789.* Boston: Houghton, Mifflin and Co., 1800.

Wilkins, Harold Tom. *Captain Kidd and his Skeleton Island.* New York: Liveright Publishing Corp., 1934.

Winchester, Simon. *Atlantic.* New York: Harper Collins, 2010.

Winston, Alexander. *No Man Knows My Grave: Privateers and Pirates 1665–1715.* Boston: Houghton Mifflin, 1969.

Woodward, Colin. *The Republic of Pirates.* New York: Harcourt, 2007.

_____. "The Last Days of Blackbeard." *Smithsonian* (February, 2014): 32–41.

Zacks, Richard. *The Pirate Hunter.* New York: Hyperion, 2002.

Index